DRUNK DRIVING LAW

by

Margaret C. Jasper, Esq.

Oceana's Legal Almanac Series:
Law for the Layperson

1999
Oceana Publications, Inc.
Dobbs Ferry, N.Y.

Information contained in this work has been obtained by Oceana Publications from sources believed to be reliable. However, neither the Publisher nor its authors guarantee the accuracy or completeness of any information published herein, and neither Oceana nor its authors shall be responsible for any errors, omissions or damages arising from the use of this information. This work is published with the understanding that Oceana and its authors are supplying information, but are not attempting to render legal or other professional services. If such services are required, the assistance of an appropriate professional should be sought.

You may order this or any other Oceana publications by visiting Oceana's Web Site at http://www.oceanalaw.com

Library of Congress Cataloging-in-Publication Data

Jasper, Margaret C.
  Drunk driving law / by Margaret C. Jasper.
      p. cm.— (Oceana's legal almanac series. Law for the layperson)
  Includes bibliographical references.
  ISBN 0-379-11336-8 (acid-free paper)
  1. Drunk driving—United States—Popular works.
I. Title. II. Series.
KF2231.Z9J37 1999
345.73'0247—dc21   99-28463
                                                                            CIP

Oceana's Legal Almanac Series: Law for the Layperson
ISSN 1075-7376

To My Husband Chris

**Your love and support
are my motivation and inspiration**

-and-

In memory of my son, Jimmy

Other Volumes Available in the Series

For more information or to order call: 1-914-693-8100
or visit us at www.oceanalaw.com

ABOUT THE AUTHOR

MARGARET C. JASPER is an attorney engaged in the general practice of law in South Salem, New York, concentrating in the areas of personal injury and entertainment law. Ms. Jasper holds a Juris Doctor degree from Pace University School of Law, White Plains, New York, is a member of the New York and Connecticut bars, and is certified to practice before the United States District Courts for the Southern and Eastern Districts of New York, and the United States Supreme Court. Ms. Jasper has been appointed to the panel of arbitrators of the American Arbitration Association and the law guardian panel for the Family Court of the State of New York, is a member of the Association of Trial Lawyers of America, and is a New York State licensed real estate broker and member of the Westchester County Board of Realtors, operating as Jasper Real Estate, in South Salem, New York.

Ms. Jasper is the author and general editor of the following legal almanacs: Juvenile Justice and Children's Law; Marriage and Divorce; Estate Planning; The Law of Contracts; The Law of Dispute Resolution; Law for the Small Business Owner; The Law of Personal Injury; Real Estate Law for the Homeowner and Broker; Everyday Legal Forms; Dictionary of Selected Legal Terms; The Law of Medical Malpractice; The Law of Product Liability; The Law of No-Fault Insurance; The Law of Immigration; The Law of Libel and Slander; The Law of Buying and Selling; Elder Law; The Right to Die; AIDS Law; The Law of Obscenity and Pornography; The Law of Child Custody; The Law of Debt Collection; Consumer Rights Law; Bankruptcy Law for the Individual Debtor; Victim's Rights Law; Animal Rights Law; Workers' Compensation Law; Employee Rights in the Workplace; Probate Law; Environmental Law; Labor Law; The Americans with Disabilities Act; The Law of Capital Punishment; Education Law; The Law of Violence Against Women; Landlord-Tenant Law; Insurance Law; Religion and the Law; Commercial Law; Motor Vehicle Law; and Social Security Law.

TABLE OF CONTENTS

INTRODUCTION

Laws designed to prevent drunk driving have been on the books in all jurisdictions for many years, some dating back to the time the automobile first made its appearance. Due in large part to strong enforcement initiatives and public awareness campaigns seeking to strengthen these laws, the incidence of alcohol-impaired driving has been reduced in recent years. Nevertheless, drinking and driving is still a major safety problem.

A number of national organizations have emerged to join in the effort to stop drunk driving, including Mothers Against Drunk Driving (MADD); Students Against Drunk Driving (SADD); and the National Commission Against Drunk Driving (NCADD). These national organizations have been founded to increase public awareness of the dangers of drunk driving. They have successfully lobbied state legislatures to stiffen penalties to punish and deter drunk driving in an effort to prevent a second or subsequent offense.

This almanac sets forth a general discussion of the law as it applies to drunk driving, including the elements of the drunk driving offense and the scope of the problem, blood alcohol concentration levels and testing, applicable laws for young drivers, victims' rights, and the penalties one may be subjected to if convicted of drunk driving. The federal legislative programs designed to reduce drunk driving are also explored. Because the law differs among jurisdictions, the reader is advised to check the law of his or her jurisdiction for specific information.

The Appendices provide relevant laws and other pertinent information and data. The drunk driving law as contained in the Uniform Vehicle Code is also set forth in the Appendix and explored herein. The Glossary contains definitions of many of the terms used throughout the almanac.

CHAPTER 1:

SCOPE OF THE PROBLEM

Overview

According to the National Traffic Safety Administration (NHTSA), almost 1.4 million people have died in traffic crashes in the United States since 1966. During the late 1960's and early 1970's, more than 50,000 people lost their lives each year on the nation's public roads and highways, and more than half of the drivers killed had been drinking.

Because traffic safety has improved since that time, in large part due to legislation which created the NHTSA in 1966, the annual death rate has declined considerably, to about 40,000, even though the number of drivers, vehicles and miles driven have all greatly increased. As reported by the NHTSA, the fatality rate per 100 million vehicle miles traveled fell from 5.5 in 1966 to 1.7 in 1996, which is a 69% improvement over three decades. Using miles traveled as a measuring stick, the likelihood of being killed in a traffic accident in 1966 was more than three times what it is today.

Nevertheless, despite these dramatic improvements in traffic safety, an average of more than 115 people still die each day from motor vehicle accidents in the United States, and it is estimated that 41 percent of the drivers who die in crashes have been drinking.

Drinking and driving is the most frequently committed violent crime in America. In the past decade, four times as many Americans died in drunk driving crashes as were killed in the Vietnam War. Between 1982 and 1995, approximately 300,274 persons lost their lives in alcohol-related traffic crashes.

According to the NHTSA, somebody dies in an alcohol-related crash every thirty minutes. It is estimated that about two in every five Americans will be involved in an alcohol-related crash at some time in their lives. The NHTSA also estimates that one out of every 280 babies born today will die in an automobile accident with an intoxicated driver. In fact, traffic crashes are the major cause of death for children age 0–14, and 21.4 percent of those deaths are alcohol-related.

A table depicting the percent of fatally injured drivers with BACs at or above 0.10 percent from 1980 to 1997, is set forth at Appendix 1.

Drinking and driving-related injuries and fatalities have become so prevalent that concerted efforts to combat the problem have increased over the last decade. Many organizations have emerged to increase public aware-ness, and have successfully lobbied for the passage and enforcement of more stringent drunk driving laws. In fact, according to the NHTSA, more than 2,300 anti-drunk driving laws have been passed since 1980.

As a result of these efforts, there has been a significant decrease in alco-hol-related traffic fatalities over the last ten years. According to the NHTSA, in 1986, there were 24,050 alcohol-related fatalities compared to 16,189 in 1997—a 32% decrease. Nevertheless, despite recent efforts to deter drunk driving, alcohol-related traffic fatalities still pose a grave and dangerous problem.

In 1997, 16,189 people were killed in alcohol-related accidents. These deaths constituted approximately 38.6% of the total 41,967 traffic fatalities for the year. In addition to the fatalities, approximately 1,058,990 people were injured in alcohol-related accidents—an average of one person injured every 30 seconds. Due to these accidents, approximately 30,000 people a year suffer permanent work-related disabilities.

A table depicting the total number of traffic-related fatalities in 1997, by state, and the number and percentage of the total which were alcohol-re-lated, is set forth at Appendix 2.

Common Misconceptions about Alcohol Impairment

Alcohol impairment is a known contributor to motor vehicle accidents. It is a misconception, however, that one must be "drunk" in order to be a dan-gerous driver. Many alcohol-impaired drivers do not appear visibly drunk. Studies have indicated that even small amounts of alcohol can impair driv-ing skills.

Another common misbelief is that the likelihood of impairment is contin-gent on the type of drink. Some mistakenly believe that beer, for instance, is less likely to cause impairment compared to hard liquor. However, impair-ment is not determined by the type of drink. It is measured by the amount of alcohol ingested over a specific period of time. In fact, beer is the most com-mon drink consumed by people stopped for alcohol-impaired driving or in-volved in alcohol-related crashes.

Many believe that they have had enough time to "sober up" between the time they drink and the time they drive, and are unaware of how much time is actually needed for one's body to metabolize alcohol. Studies indicate that most people need at least one hour to metabolize one drink.

Drug Use and Driving

There is much less information concerning the role of drugs in motor vehicle accidents as compared to alcohol. It is established, however, that many legal and illegal drugs can impair driving ability, even in moderate concentrations, and may increase the risk of accidents. However, there is presently insufficient scientific evidence concerning the effect of drugs, other than alcohol, on driving.

According to a 1988 NHTSA report, the drugs with the most potential to be serious highway safety hazards are tranquilizers, sedatives and hypnotics. However, it is difficult to ascertain what contribution drugs have made in motor vehicle crashes. Information on a driver's drug use typically comes from hospital tests performed on people who are killed in crashes or hospitalized with crash injuries.

A 1992 federal study revealed that eighteen percent of fatally injured drivers have other drugs in their systems but that these drugs are most often combined with alcohol. Alcohol was found in fifty-two percent of 1,882 fatally injured drivers. Forty-three percent had blood alcohol concentrations of 0.10 percent or more. Only six percent had drugs without alcohol, and researchers found no evidence that drivers with drugs but no alcohol are more likely to be responsible for their crashes, compared with drug-free drivers. The researchers did find that drugs were related to crash responsibility when combined with alcohol, or when two or more drugs were found.

Nevertheless, the use of stimulants by tractor-trailer drivers has become a noteworthy problem. A National Transportation Safety Board (NTSB) investigation of fatal truck crashes found that stimulants were the most frequently identified drug class among fatally injured drivers, and were present in approximately 15 percent of those drivers.

Studies have been undertaken to assess the effect of stimulants. It has been found that occasional use of stimulants may, in the short term, enhance the performance of some tasks by increasing alertness. However, some tractor-trailer drivers may use these drugs to continue on the road for prolonged periods. Use of stimulants for this purpose is probably frequent and sustained, not occasional, and thus is potentially dangerous.

Costs

According to the NHTSA, automobile crashes claim about 42,000 lives each year in the United States. The associated costs to society are overwhelming: economic costs ($150 billion including $19 billion in medical care and emergency expenses); lost productivity ($42 billion); property damage ($52 billion); and miscellaneous crash-related costs ($37 billion). Approximately thirty percent of these automobile accidents are alcohol-related, accounting for $45 billion in associated costs each year. This figure does not include pain, suffering and lost quality of life, which significantly raise that figure.

The cost for each injured survivor of an alcohol-related crash averaged $67,000, including $6,000 in health care costs and $13,000 in lost productivity. In addition, over 25 percent of the first year of medical costs for persons hospitalized as a result of an automobile crash are paid by tax dollars, about two-thirds through Medicaid and one-third through Medicare.

Gender and Age

Accidents involving men are much more likely to be alcohol-related than those involving women. Among fatally injured male drivers of passenger vehicles in 1997, 37 percent had BACs of 0.10 percent or more and were age 31-40. The corresponding proportion among women was 17 percent, the majority of which fell in the same age group.

Since 1980, the proportion of fatally injured passenger vehicle drivers with BACs at or above 0.10 percent declined more among drivers 16-20 years of age than among older drivers.

A table depicting the percent of fatally injured passenger vehicle drivers with BACs at or above 0.10 percent, by gender and age, for 1997, is set forth at Appendix 3.

Time of Day

Alcohol-related accidents may occur at any time of day, however, the incidence peaks at night and increases on weekends and holidays. According to the Insurance Institute for Highway Safety (IIHS), in 1997, 66 percent of passenger vehicle drivers with BACs at or above 0.10 percent were fatally injured between midnight and 3 a.m., compared with 7 percent between 9 am and noon.

A table depicting the percent of fatally injured passenger vehicle drivers with BACs at or above 0.10 percent, by time of day, for 1997, is set forth at Appendix 4.

In addition, forty-three percent of all drivers fatally injured on the weekends—defined as 6 p.m. Friday to 6 a.m. Monday—had BACs of 0.10 percent or more. During the rest of the week, the proportion was twenty-three percent.

According to the NHTSA, in single-vehicle crashes occurring on weekend nights in 1994, 72.3% of the fatally injured drivers 25 years of age or older were intoxicated, as compared with 57.7% of drivers under the age of 25.

Holiday periods also account for a disproportionate number of alcohol-related traffic accidents. As may be expected, of all the accidents which occurred on New Years Eve/Day in 1997, the largest percentage were alcohol-related (67%).

A table depicting the total number of traffic-related fatalities during holiday periods in 1997, and the number and percentage of the total which were alcohol-related, is set forth at Appendix 5.

Type of Vehicle

According to IIHS statistics, since 1980, the percentage of fatally injured people with BACs at or above 0.10 percent has declined among passenger vehicle drivers, tractor-trailer drivers and motorcyclists. In 1980, the proportion of passenger vehicle driver deaths involving BACs at or above 0.10 percent was 54 percent, compared with 31 percent for 1997, and the proportion of motorcyclist deaths involving BACs at or above 0.10 percent was 46 percent in 1980, compared with 34 percent in 1997.

The group of drivers with the greatest decline in alcohol-related fatalities is tractor-trailer drivers. In 1980, the proportion of fatally injured tractor-trailer drivers with BACs at or above 0.10 percent was 15 percent, compared with 3 percent in 1997.

BAC Levels

As further set forth in Chapter 3, many states are lowering their BAC to define impaired driving from 0.10 percent to 0.08 percent, based on studies demonstrating the sharp decline in driving ability above this level.

According to the IIHS, the probability of an automobile crash begins to significantly increase at 0.05 percent BAC and climbs rapidly after 0.08 percent BAC. Among drivers with BACs above 0.15 percent, the likelihood of dying in a single-vehicle crash during weekend nights is more than 380 times higher than for drivers who do not drink.

Many states have also enacted "zero tolerance" laws which set the BAC for young drivers even lower—0.00 to 0.02 percent—in large part based on studies showing a BAC as low as 0.02 percent negatively impacts driving ability. Zero tolerance laws have been found to reduce the incidence of alcohol-related automobile crashes involving young drivers by twenty percent.

DUI/DWI Arrests and Convictions

According to the FBI, arrests for driving while under the influence (DUI) and driving while impaired (DWI) resulted in one of the highest arrest counts categorized in 1994—at 1.4 million—the same number of arrests for drug abuse violations and slightly higher than arrests for larcenies (1.5 million). In addition, of the 14.6 million arrests for criminal infractions in 1994, driving under the influence was the offense most often committed by adults.

According to the NHTSA, even though there was a two percent decline in the national crime rate during the cited period, the number of arrests for driving under the influence increased from 1.2 million in 1993 to 1.4 million in 1994—an arrest rate of one for every 127 licensed drivers in the United States. Further, approximately one-third of all drivers arrested for DWI are repeat offenders. According to the Bureau of Justice Statistics (BJS), almost nine out of ten DWI offenders in jail—86%—had previously been sentenced to probation, jail or prison for DWI or for other offenses.

Of the total DWI offenders sentenced to jail in 1993, the median term imposed was six months. Those offenders with two or more prior DWI sentences received sentences more than 1.3 times longer than first-time offenders.

According to the BJS, prior to their DWI arrest, one-half of the convicted offenders in jail had consumed at least six ounces of pure alcohol in the space of 5 hours, and approximately 29% had consumed at least 11 ounces of pure alcohol.

According to the FBI, arrests of youths under the age of 18 significantly increased from 1984 to 1993 for drunkenness (42.9%); DUI (50.2%); and drug abuse (27.8%). In addition, of all persons arrested for DUI/DWI nationally in 1993, persons in the under 25 age group accounted for 23.4% of those in the cities, 23.7% of those in the suburban counties, and 22.1% of those in rural counties.

CHAPTER 2:

ELEMENTS OF THE DRUNK DRIVING OFFENSE

In General

All jurisdictions have drunk driving statutes. This chapter provides an overview of the basic elements of drunk driving common to most state statutes. Although all of the statutes contain similar provisions, the broad terms used to describe the elements of the offense of drunk driving have subjected them to differing judicial interpretations. Thus, the reader is advised to check both the statute and case law of his or her jurisdiction when researching a particular issue.

Use of the Vehicle

The statutory construction used to describe the use of the vehicle in the crime of drunk driving differs among jurisdictions, although all jurisdictions include either the term "driving" or "operating" a motor vehicle as an essential element of the crime of drunk driving. For example, West Virginia specifies "drives" as the use of the vehicle. (W. Va. Code §17C-5-2), while Connecticut describes the necessary use of the vehicle as to "operate." (Conn. Gen. Stat. Ann. §14-227a). Mississippi uses both terms, describing the necessary use as "to drive or otherwise operate." (Miss. Code Ann. § 63-11-30).

The term "driving" has been interpreted in the most narrowest sense, and generally requires the vehicle to be in motion. The term "operating" is more broad, and has been interpreted to include starting the engine or manipulating the mechanical or electrical devices of a standing vehicle.

Section 11-902 of the Uniform Vehicle Code, from which many jurisdictions have adopted language in full or in part for their own drunk driving statutes, describes the requisite act as being in "actual physical control," in conjunction with the term "driving":

> (a) A person shall not drive or be in *actual physical control* of any vehicle while (1) the alcohol concentration in such person's blood or breath is 0.08 or more . . .

For example, Idaho describes the use of vehicle element as to "drive or be in actual physical control." (Idaho Code §18-8004). Minnesota's statute includes all of the above, describing the necessary use as to "drive, operate, or be in physical control." (Minn. Stat. Ann. § 169.121).

This statutory description is more inclusive than either "driving" or "operating." Actual physical control generally does not require the vehicle to be moving. For example, the Illinois Court of Appeals has applied this definition to an individual who is seated behind the steering wheel with the ignition key and physically capable of starting the engine and moving the vehicle.

Selected provisions of the Uniform Vehicle Code related to drunk driving are set forth at Appendix 6.

Evidence of Driving, Operating or Actual Physical Control

Oftentimes, there is no direct evidence that an individual was driving, operating, or in control of a vehicle. For example, following a one-car accident, there are generally no witnesses, and the driver has likely exited the car. Although the driver may admit to the police that he was driving the vehicle, there must also be some evidence independent of the driver's admission because evidence of driving is an "essential element" of the crime. The driver's admission alone has been held insufficient to convict absent some corroboration.

Circumstantial evidence may be used to corroborate the driver's admission. For example, if the driver hit her head on the windshield upon impact, and there is blood matching the driver's blood type found on the glass, this may serve to corroborate the driver's admission. The independent evidence need not prove the act beyond a reasonable doubt provided it tends to confirm the driver's admission.

If the driver does not admit to driving the vehicle, circumstantial evidence may be the only evidence available to the prosecution, and has been held to be sufficient to convict in a drunk driving case. Convictions have been upheld in cases where, for example, the defendant was seen driving the vehicle a short time prior to the accident; or the defendant was found sleeping behind the wheel and the engine, although not running, was still warm.

Type of Vehicle

In general, all jurisdictions include automobiles, trucks and motorcycles as types of vehicles covered under their drunk driving law. Many jurisdictions parallel the language of the Uniform Vehicle Code, which simply uses the term "any vehicle":

> (a) A person shall not drive or be in actual physical control of *any vehicle* while (1) the alcohol concentration in such person's blood or breath is 0.08 or more . . .

One must also be aware of judicial interpretations of the statutory term. In general, if the statute uses the term "motor vehicle," it refers to vehicles which are equipped with a motor. Thus, less traditional forms of transportation, such as a a moped or snowmobile, may be covered under the statute. However, a statute which merely uses the term "vehicle," may be interpreted more broadly by a court to include a bicycle. In fact, a North Carolina court has interpreted its statute to prohibit drunken horseback riding.

Location of Offense

Section 11-901.1(a) of the Uniform Vehicle Code makes it unlawful to drive drunk "within" or "in" the state. Many states also use this terminology in defining the places where drunk driving is prohibited. Because the intent is to protect the public from harm, the statutes generally apply to public highways and roads and areas open to the public, including private property, such as parking lots.

For example, New York's drunk driving statute defines the applicable locations as follows:

Where applicable. The provisions of this section shall apply upon public highways, private roads open to motor vehicle traffic and any other parking lot. For the purposes of this section "parking lot" shall mean any area or areas of private property, including a driveway, near or contiguous to and provided in connection with premises and used as a means of access to and egress from a public highway to such premises and having a capacity for the parking of four or more motor vehicles. The provisions of this section shall not apply to any area or areas of private property comprising all or part of property on which is situated a one or two family residence.
(N.Y. Veh. & Traf. Law § 1192(7)).

Some statutes do not specify locations where drunk driving is prohibited in the statute, relying on the language that drunk driving is prohibited anywhere "in the state." Such statutes have been interpreted literally and thus have resulted in drunk driving convictions regardless of the location provided the offense occurred within the state.

Unless the statute is one which does not specify actual locations where drunk driving is prohibited, the location of the offense is an element of the crime that must be proven by the prosecution. Generally, location is proven through eyewitness testimony or circumstantial evidence.

Intoxication and Illegal Per Se Statutes

Proof of intoxication generally requires the prosecutor to prove that the driver consumed enough alcohol to satisfy the jurisdiction's legal definition of intoxication. The statutes of nearly all jurisdictions also contain a clause prohibiting driving while under the influence of drugs.

To address the difficulty of meeting the standard of "intoxication," most jurisdictions have created an "illegal per se" blood alcohol concentration (BAC) level. The statute sets a minimum blood alcohol level—e.g. 0.10 percent—which can be measured to satisfy the intoxication requirement. Thus, the prosecution does not have to prove that the driver was "intoxicated" or "under the influence," or that alcohol consumption had any effect on the driver's ability to operate the vehicle.

For example, New York's illegal per se statute states:

Driving while intoxicated; per se. No person shall operate a motor vehicle while such person has .10 of one per centum or more by weight of alcohol in the person's blood as shown by chemical analysis of such person's blood, breath, urine or saliva, made pursuant to the provisions of section eleven hundred ninety-four of this article. (N.Y. Veh. & Traf. Law §1192(2)).

The Uniform Vehicle Code has adopted 0.08 percent as the per se illegal BAC limit:

SECTION 11-902. Driving while under the influence of alcohol or drugs.

(a) A person shall not drive or be in actual physical control of any vehicle while:

1. The alcohol concentration in such person's blood or breath is 0.08 or more based on the definition of blood and breath units in §11-903(a) (5).

The topic of blood alcohol concentration (BAC) levels and the systems used to measure a driver's BAC level is more fully set forth in Chapter 3.

Intoxication While Driving

It is not enough to merely establish that the driver was intoxicated. It is also necessary to establish that the driver was intoxicated *while* he or she was driving or operating the vehicle. For example, a driver involved in a one-car accident may claim that her intoxication resulted from her drinking after the accident occurred, particularly where considerable time has elapsed between the accident and the arrival of police.

Intent

In order to convict, the prosecution does not have to prove that the driver had any specific intent—i.e., mens rea—to drive while intoxicated. Proof of a general intent to drink and then proceed to drive is all that is required. Thus, the driver need not be aware that he is under the influence of alcohol while driving in order to be convicted provided he consumed alcoholic beverages and thereafter intentionally drove.

CHAPTER 3:

BLOOD ALCOHOL CONCENTRATION LEVEL

In General

The primary indicator of whether a person has had too much to drink is their blood alcohol concentration (BAC) level. The BAC describes the concentration of alcohol in a person's blood expressed as weight per unit of volume. For example, at 0.10 percent BAC, there is a concentration of 100 mg of alcohol per 100 ml of blood. BAC measurements provide an objective way to identify levels of impairment, because alcohol concentration in the body is directly related to impairment.

Because the rate that alcohol is absorbed into the blood differs from person to person based on such factors as age, weight and gender, the effect that alcohol will have on a particular person varies greatly. Other factors, such as the amount of food in the stomach, also affect alcohol absorption. Therefore, it is difficult to determine exactly how many drinks will result in a heightened BAC.

Illegal Per Se Statutes

The first state drunk driving laws generally prohibited driving while intoxicated or while under the influence of alcohol. In practical terms, this meant that only obviously impaired drivers—so-called drunks—were likely to be arrested and, even then, it was difficult to obtain a conviction because no objective standard existed to prove intoxication. When the relationship between BACs and impairment of skills was established, it became possible to define offenses in terms of a BAC above a defined threshold.

Every state law now uses BAC results to prosecute offenders. Initially, this was done through laws that established a rebuttable presumption of impairment at or above a specified BAC. Now 48 states and the District of Columbia have "illegal per se" laws defining the offense as driving with a BAC above a proscribed limit, similar to a speed limit. Thus, it is against the law to drive a vehicle with a BAC at or above the illegal per se limit, even if the driver exhibits no visible signs of intoxication. In most states, the proscribed level is 0.10 percent, although there is a concerted effort by the federal government to have a uniform illegal per se limit of 0.08 percent.

The push for a 0.08 percent BAC limit is based on laboratory and on-road research which demonstrates that the majority of drivers, regardless of experience, are significantly impaired at 0.08 percent BAC, and show a critical decline in their ability to perform critical driving tasks, such as braking, steering, lane changing, judgment, and divided attention. In fact, research suggests that the most critical aspect of impairment is the reduction in the ability to handle several tasks at once, a skill motor vehicle drivers must perform.

A table of state illegal per se BAC levels applicable to all drivers is set forth at Appendix 7.

Young Drivers

Forty-five states and the District of Columbia have set their BAC limit for young drivers—i.e., drivers under the age of 21—much lower. These statutes are known as "zero tolerance" laws, which generally provide BAC limits at 0.02 percent or lower. The topic of alcohol use among young drivers is discussed further in Chapter 5 of this almanac.

A table of state illegal per se BAC levels applicable to young drivers is set forth at Appendix 8.

Standard of Proof

A "per se" violation needs no further corroboration. The BAC in and of itself is proof that the law was violated. Defendants can no longer try to prove they were not impaired, although they can challenge the validity of the BAC tests.

For example, the Uniform Vehicle Code prohibits driving at or above 0.08 percent:

> (a) A person shall not drive or be in actual physical control of any vehicle while (1) the alcohol concentration in such person's blood or breath is 0.08 or more . . . (U.V.C. § 11-902).

Driving with a BAC of 0.10 percent is a crime in 33 states and the District of Columbia, and evidence of an alcohol violation in South Carolina. It is a crime to drive with a BAC of 0.08 percent in 15 states, and an alcohol violation in Massachusetts.

Relationship Between Accidents and BAC Level

The likelihood that a driver will have an accident increases steadily at BAC levels higher than zero. Even at a BAC as low as 0.02 percent, alcohol affects driving ability. The probability of a crash begins to increase significantly at 0.05 percent BAC and climbs rapidly after about 0.08 percent.

Although drivers with BACs at or above 0.10 percent represent only 17 percent of all drinking drivers on weekend nights, they represent 87 percent of the fatally injured drivers who had been drinking during those time periods. In fact, studies indicate that for drivers with BACs above 0.15 percent on weekend nights, the likelihood of being killed in a single-vehicle crash is more than 380 times higher than it is for nondrinking drivers.

Although alcohol is known to increase crash likelihood, its presence is neither necessary nor sufficient to cause a crash. Every crash in which a driver has a high BAC is not caused by alcohol. Nevertheless, statistics have demonstrated that a large percentage of drivers who are fatally injured have a BAC of at least 0.10 percent.

According to a 1996 NHTSA study, 32 percent of all traffic deaths occurred in crashes in which at least one driver had a BAC of 0.10 percent or more. The incidence of alcohol involvement is much lower in crashes involving nonfatal injuries, and it is lower still in crashes that do not involve injuries at all.

CHAPTER 4:

BAC DETECTION METHODS

In General

Although police cannot stop and test individual drivers without cause, they can investigate any driver who, based on established criteria, appears to have been driving while impaired by alcohol. As further set forth below, most alcohol-impaired driving arrests are made by officers on routine patrol who discern signs of impairment after stopping a driver for an ordinary traffic violation. This chapter discusses the right of law enforcement officers to stop drivers suspected of drinking and driving, and the testing methods law enforcement officers employ to determine whether a driver is alcohol-impaired.

Chemical Testing

The term *blood* alcohol concentration is somewhat misleading because a blood sample is not necessary to determine a person's BAC. The simplest way to test a person's BAC is by analyzing exhaled breath—a "breathalyzer" test—the primary method of testing used by law enforcement agencies. A person's BAC level can also be measured by testing their urine or saliva. Most states provide that any one of the foregoing samples are admissible as proof of intoxication.

For example, the Indiana drunk driving statute provides:

> Scope of Use of Chemical Test Results. At any proceeding concerning an offense under IC 9-30-5 or a violation under IC 9-30-15, evidence of the amount by weight of alcohol that was in the blood of the person charged with the offense (1) at the time of the alleged violation; or (2) within the time allowed for testing under IC 9-30-6-2, *as shown by an analysis of the person's breath, blood or urine or other bodily substance,* is admissible. (Ind. Code Ann. § 9-30-6-3).

A passive alcohol sensor is a common device used by law enforcement officers at roadside stops. The passive alcohol sensor is non-invasive and can be performed even if the driver remains in his or her vehicle. Breath testing equipment is evaluated for precision and accuracy by the National Highway Traffic Safety Administration (NHTSA), and must be accurate within plus or minus .005 of the true BAC value to meet NHTSA approval.

Nevertheless, the most accurate and direct determination of one's BAC is obtained through an analysis of a blood sample. Advantages of a blood sample over other types of BAC testing is that it is relatively inexpensive and can be taken by a number of qualified persons who are generally available, there is reduced likelihood that the person administering the test can interfere with the results, and a blood sample, unlike a breath analysis, can be saved indefinitely. The disadvantages are that it takes longer to obtain the results of a blood test, and the procedure is more invasive and carries certain health risks.

Implied Consent Statutes and the Refusal to Submit to BAC Testing

A driver who has been drinking and is subsequently stopped for suspicion of drunk driving may be understandably reluctant to submit to BAC testing, because the results of the test may be all that is needed for a conviction. Because BAC testing provides a clear advantage to the prosecution, and assists states in making sure their roads are free from drunk drivers, implied consent laws have been enacted to deter the drunk driver's incentive to refuse to submit to BAC testing.

Implied consent statutes generally provide for automatic suspension of the license of any driver who refuses to submit to BAC testing. In some states, evidence of refusal is admissible at trial, and may be the basis for an enhanced sentence if the driver is convicted on the drunk driving offense. Nevertheless, an implied consent statute generally requires that the law enforcement officer have some reasonable basis or probable cause to believe that the driver was operating under the influence before he requests the driver to submit to a test.

Some states give drivers the statutory right to consult with an attorney before making the decision whether or not to submit to BAC testing. However, this right is not absolute and will be limited if the driver is unable to contact an attorney within a reasonable period of time. If, however, the police fail to advise the driver of his or her right to contact an attorney, in jurisdictions where notice is required, the results of any police-administered test may be suppressed.

A table of states which have enacted mandatory BAC level testing is set forth at Appendix 9.

Section 6-207 of the Uniform Vehicle Code sets forth a typical implied consent provision:

SECTION 6-207(a). Any person who operates a motor vehicle upon the highways of this State shall be deemed to have given consent, subject to the provisions of § 11-903, to a test or tests of such operator's blood, breath, or urine for the purpose of determining operator's alcohol concentration or the presence of other drugs. The test or tests shall be administered at the direction of a law enforcement officer who has probable cause to believe the person has been violating § 11-902(a), and one of the following conditions exists:

1. The person has been arrested for violating § 11-902(a) or any other offense alleged to have been committed while the person was violating § 11-902(a);

2. The person has been involved in an accident;

3. The person has refused to submit to the preliminary screening test authorized by § 6-209; or

4. The person has submitted to the preliminary screening test authorized by § 6-209 which disclosed an alcohol concentration of 0.08 or more.

Most jurisdictions provide that the license of a driver who refuses to submit to BAC testing is subject to mandatory suspension or revocation. The Uniform Vehicle Code also provides that drivers who refuse to submit to testing, or who have tested at or above 0.08 percent are subject to license revocation

SECTION 6-207(c). A person requested to submit to a test as provided above shall be warned by the law enforcement officer requesting the test that a refusal to submit to the test will result in revocation of such person's license to operate a motor vehicle for (six months) (one year).

Suspensions are imposed primarily to protect the public from intoxicated drivers rather than merely a form of punishment for the driver. Although many offenders continue to drive after having their licenses suspended, many studies have indicated that the suspensions reduce recidivism compared with offenders whose licenses are not suspended. In addition, the reductions in violations and crashes associated with license suspension continue well beyond the suspension period.

Driver's Right to Chemical Test

A sober driver accused of driving while impaired may wish to clear his name by obtaining an independent chemical test to use as exculpatory evidence of sobriety. Many states allow a driver to undergo a second test once he or she has submitted to the test requested by a law enforcement officer. Some states have held that a driver has the right to an independent test whether or not he or she submitted to the initial test. However, a police officer is generally not under any duty to advise the driver of his or her right to an independent test unless the statute explicitly requires him to do so.

The initial police-administered test is generally a breath test. However, the most common privately administered test is a blood test due to it accuracy. Unfortunately, as a practical matter, a driver who is arrested late at night may not be able to obtain a blood test. If the police give the driver the opportunity to obtain an independent test, but the driver is unable to do so, the initial police-administered test is nonetheless admissible against the driver.

For example, Alabama's drunk driving law provides:

The person tested may at his own expense have a physician, or a qualified technician, registered nurse or other qualified person of his own choosing administer a chemical test or tests in addition to any administered at the discretion of a law enforcement officer. The failure or inability to obtain an additional test by a person shall not preclude the admission of evidence relating to the test or tests taken at the direction of a law enforcement officer. (Ala. CODE 32-5-192).

Nevertheless, if the police refuse to allow the driver to obtain an independent test, the initial test results may not be admissible.

Sobriety Checkpoints

Some jurisdictions have their officers working exclusively on enforcing alcohol-related laws. In that connection, they may set up sobriety checkpoints at specified locations to identify impaired drivers. At the sobriety checkpoint, all drivers, or a predetermined proportion of them, are stopped based on rules that prevent police from arbitrarily selecting drivers. Sobriety checkpoints are often established at times when drinking and driving is most prevalent, such as weekends and certain holiday periods.

Checkpoints are a very visible enforcement method intended to deter potential offenders as well as to catch violators. Checkpoints that are well-publicized, and set up frequently over long enough periods, have proven to be effective deterrents to drivers who fear they will be apprehended if they drink and drive.

The U.S. Supreme Court held in 1990 that properly conducted sobriety checkpoints are legal under the federal Constitution. Most state courts that have addressed the issue have upheld checkpoints, too, but some have interpreted state law to prohibit checkpoints.

According to the NHTSA, two-thirds of the driving age public believe sobriety checkpoints should be used more frequently than they are now. In fact, a majority of drivers who drink are supportive of the increased use of sobriety checkpoints.

A table of states which have enacted sobriety checkpoint legislation is set forth at Appendix 10.

Visual DWI Detection of Moving Vehicles

Unlike sobriety checkpoints, which stop all or a predetermined number of drivers regardless of any visual detection of alcohol impairment, law enforcement officers also routinely stop drivers who exhibit some indication of alcohol impairment while in motion, such as weaving or coming dangerously close to stationary objects or other vehicles. According to the NHTSA, the highest probability of alcohol impairment—a 65% probability at night that the driver has a BAC of at least 0.10 percent—is associated with the actions of turning a vehicle with a wide radius or straddling a center or lane marker between the left-hand and right-hand wheels.

In addition, the law enforcement officer obtains visual cues from the manner of response when the officer requests the driver to pull over. For example, cues suggesting alcohol impairment may include a sudden stop, a swerve, contact with a stationary object, a slow or no response, or an attempt to evade police and flee the scene.

NHTSA Research and Development of BAC Evaluation Methods

An emphasis on DWI enforcement over the last two decades has resulted in a significant improvement in traffic safety, as demonstrated by a reduction in overall traffic accidents as well as those which are alcohol-related. The NHTSA has made a large contribution to this reduction in DWI by providing law enforcement officers with scientifically valid and useful information and training materials concerning DWI behaviors. In 1975, the National Highway Traffic Safety Administration (NHTSA) began sponsoring research that led to the development of standardized methods for police officers to use when evaluating drivers who are suspected of driving while impaired (DWI).

This information is the product of research sponsored by the NHTSA, which led to the development of a DWI detection guide listing 20 driving cues and the probabilities that a driver exhibiting one or more of those cues would have a BAC of at least .010 percent. A similar study recently sponsored by the NHTSA identified 24 driving cues that predict DWI at the 0.08

percent BAC level. The NHTSA has also sponsored research that led to the development of a motorcycle DWI detection guide.

In 1981, law enforcement officers began using the NHTSA's Standardized Field Sobriety Test (SFST) battery to help determine whether drivers who are suspected of DWI have blood alcohol concentrations (BACs) greater than 0.10 percent. An evaluation of a number of tests routinely given by law enforcement officers at roadside stops was made, including, for example, the finger to nose test, maze tracing, and counting backward, in addition to the driver's reaction to central nervous system depressants, known as horizontal gaze nystagmus (HGN), which is more fully described below.

Statistically, HGN tested to be the most predictive of the individual measures studied. However, the combined scores of three of the tests studied—one-leg stand, walk and turn, and horizontal gaze nystagmus—provided a slightly higher correlation to BAC than HGN alone. The combined score correctly discriminated between BACs below or above 0.10 percent in 83% of the subjects tested in the study conducted in 1977.

Upon receiving these results, the NHTSA sponsored a subsequent study to standardize the test administration and scoring procedures and conduct further evaluations of the new battery of the three tests. The research demonstrated that police officers tended to increase their arrest rates and were more effective in estimating BACs of stopped drivers after they had been trained in the administration and scoring of the Standardized Field Sobriety Test (SFST) battery.

The results of the study were documented in detail in a report entitled *Development and Field Test of Psychophysical Tests for DWI Arrest* (Tharp, Burns and Moskowitz, 1981), which has been cited numerous times throughout the United States to establish the scientific validity of the SFST battery and to support law enforcement officers' in court testimony.

The Standardized Field Sobriety Test

As discussed above, the Standardized Field Sobriety Test (SFST) has largely replaced the unvalidated performance tests once used by police officers in traffic stops to make DWI arrest decisions, and is used in all 50 states. The SFST has become the standard pre-arrest procedure for evaluating DWI by most law enforcement agencies. The SFST accurately and reliably assists trained officers in making DWI arrest decisions at 0.08 percent BAC. The SFST has also proven to be useful for making arrest decisions at 0.04 percent BAC.

As set forth above, the SFST consists of a battery of three tests which are administered and evaluated in a standardized manner to obtain valid indicators of impairment and establish probable cause for arrest: (i) horizontal gaze nystagmus (HGN); (ii) walk-and-turn; and (iii) one-leg stand.

The Horizontal Gaze Nystagmus (HGN)

Horizontal gaze nystagmus (HGN) is an involuntary jerking of one's eye that occurs naturally as the eyes gaze to the side. Under normal conditions, nystagmus occurs when the eyes are rotated at high peripheral angles. However, when a person is impaired by alcohol, nystagmus is exaggerated and may occur at lesser angles. Studies have indicated that there are consistent changes in HGN with increasing doses of alcohol.

An alcohol-impaired person will also often have difficulty smoothly tracking a moving object. In the HGN test, the officer observes the eyes of the driver as he or she follows a slowly moving object horizontally with his or her eyes. The examiner looks for three indicators of impairment in each eye:

1. If the eye cannot follow a moving object smoothly;

2. If jerking is distinct when the eye is at maximum deviation; and

3. If the angle of onset of jerking is within 45 degrees of center.

If, between the two eyes, four or more clues appear, the suspect is likely to have a BAC of 0.10 percent or greater. NHTSA research indicates that the HGN test allows proper classification of approximately 77 percent of suspects. HGN may also indicate consumption of seizure medications, phencyclidine, and a variety of inhalants, barbiturates and other depressants.

Many law enforcement officers consider the HGN test a foolproof method to provide indisputable evidence of alcohol in a driver's system. Unlike performance tests, which result in uncertainties due to the normal variation in human physical and cognitive capabilities, most experienced drinkers cannot conceal the physiological effects of alcohol from an officer trained in HGN administration. HGN is an involuntary reaction over which an individual has no control whatsoever.

Walk and Turn Test

The walk-and-turn test, as well as the one-leg stand test which is discussed below, are easily performed by most unimpaired people. They merely require a suspect to listen to and follow instructions while performing simple physical movements. However, when an individual is impaired, he or she has difficulty performing tasks which require their attention to be divided between simple mental and physical exercises.

During the walk-and-turn test, the driver is asked to take nine steps, heel to toe, along a straight line. After taking the steps, the driver must turn on one foot and return in the same manner in the opposite direction. The examiner looks for eight indicators of impairment, including:

1. If the suspect cannot keep his balance while listening to the instructions;

2. If the suspect begins before the instructions are finished;

3. If the suspect stops while walking to regain his balance;

4. If the suspect does not touch heel-to-toe;

5. If the suspect steps off the line;

6. If the suspect uses his or her arms to balance;

7. If the suspect makes an improper turn; or

8. If the suspect takes an incorrect number of steps.

The NHTSA research indicates that 68 percent of individuals who exhibit two or more indicators in the performance of the test will have a BAC of 0.10 percent or greater.

One Leg Stand

The one leg stand requires the driver to stand with one foot approximately six inches off the ground and count aloud by thousands until told to put his or her foot down. The officer times the driver for 30 seconds and looks for four indicators of impairment, including (i) swaying while balancing; (ii) using arms to balance; (iii) hopping to maintain balance; and (iv) putting one's foot down. NHTSA research indicates that 76 percent of individuals who exhibit two or more such indicators in the performance of the test will have a BAC of 0.10 of greater.

A Sample NHTSA SFST Validation Data Form is set forth at Appendix 11.

Passive Alcohol Sensors

Passive alcohol sensors identify alcohol in the exhaled breath near a driver's mouth. They are particularly effective in situations where the driver is able to effectively hide symptoms of impairment for short periods of time. Because passive alcohol sensors are not intrusive, they have been held not to violate the constitutional prohibitions against unreasonable search and seizure.

Studies conducted by the Insurance Institute for Highway Safety have indicated that police using these sensors were able to detect more offenders compared with officers who did not use the sensors. Police without sensors detected 55 percent of drivers whose BACs were at or above 0.10 percent whereas police with sensors successfully detected 71 percent of the drivers with illegal BACs.

CHAPTER 5:

ALCOHOL USE AND YOUNG DRIVERS

In General

As a group, teenage drivers are disproportionately involved in motor vehicle crashes worldwide. In 1996, 5,805 teenagers died in the United States from motor vehicle crash injuries. Such injuries are by far the leading public health problem for young people 13-19 years old. Thirty-four percent of all deaths of 16-19 year-olds from all causes are related to motor vehicles.

In addition to teenage drivers, many teenagers die as passengers in motor vehicles. Sixty-three percent of teenage passenger deaths in 1996 occurred in crashes in which another teenager was driving. Teenagers far exceed all other age groups in terms of per capita deaths as both drivers and passengers, but their passenger fatality rates are much more extreme compared with those of older drivers.

A number of factors have been found to contribute to the high incidence of accidents involving younger drivers, including driver error; speeding; failure to use seat belts; high occupancy vehicles; and alcohol use.

Alcohol use is the number one drug problem among young people. In 1995, statistics indicated that about 10 million drinkers were under the age of 21, 4.4 million of which were binge drinkers and 1.7 million of which were considered heavy drinkers. According to a 1991 report by the U.S. Surgeon General, more than half of the nation's junior and senior high school students—the age of beginner drivers—drink alcoholic beverages, and many "binge" drink to relieve stress and boredom.

Alcohol Use as a Factor in Automobile Accidents

Although young drivers are less likely than adults to drive after drinking alcohol, their crash risks are substantially higher when they do. This is especially true at low and moderate blood alcohol concentrations (BACs) and is thought to result from teenagers' relative inexperience with both drinking and driving.

Statistically, approximately eight young people a day die in alcohol-related crashes. According to the National Highway Traffic Safety Administration (NHTSA), more than 40% of all 16–20 year old deaths result from motor vehicle crashes, and approximately one-half of those accidents are alcohol-related. In 1994, it is estimated that 2,222 young people aged 16-20 died in alcohol-related crashes.

Minimum Alcohol Purchasing Age Laws

Minimum alcohol purchasing age laws have been effective in reducing alcohol-related accidents involving teenagers, and many communities are strengthening enforcement of these laws. For a long time, the legal age for purchasing alcohol was 21 years old in the majority of states. Then, in the 1960s and early 1970s, many states lowered their minimum purchasing ages to 18 or 19 years old.

According to the Insurance Institute for Highway Safety, the consequences of this action resulted in an increase in the number of 15-20 year-olds involved in nighttime fatal crashes. As a result of this and other studies with similar findings, a number of states raised their minimum alcohol purchasing ages. Some states reverted back to 21 years old, and other states set 19 or 20 as the minimum age. Subsequent research indicated that states which raised their minimum legal alcohol purchasing age experienced a 13 percent reduction in nighttime driver fatal crash involvement involving teenagers.

In 1984, 23 states had minimum alcohol purchasing ages of 21 years old. Federal legislation was enacted to withhold highway funds from the remaining 27 states if they did not follow suit. Since July 1988, all 50 states and the District of Columbia have required alcohol purchasers to be 21 years old.

According to the NHTSA, fatal crashes among young drivers declined dramatically as states adopted older purchasing ages, and by 1996 the statistic had declined to 24 percent, the biggest improvement for any age group. In fact, between 1985 and 1995, the proportion of drivers aged 16-20 who were involved in fatal crashes, and were intoxicated, dropped 47 percent, the largest decrease or any age group during this period.

Zero Tolerance Laws

Forty-eight jurisdictions have established very low legal BAC thresholds—known as "zero tolerance laws"—for young drivers. Zero tolerance laws make it illegal for drivers under the age of 21 to drive with any measurable amount of alcohol in their system, despite the BAC limit established for older drivers.

The reasoning and justification behind zero tolerance laws is the illegality of persons under the age of 21 to purchase or publicly possess alcohol. If it is illegal for them to purchase or possess alcohol, they certainly should not be permitted to drive after having consumed alcohol. This is particularly troublesome due to the fact that young drivers are already more likely to be involved in automobile accidents due to other factors, such as lack of experience.

As further set forth in Chapter 7 of this almanac, recent federal legislation required all states to enact zero tolerance laws for youth by October 1, 1998 or face federal sanctions. As a result, all 50 states and the District of Columbia now have zero tolerance laws.

A table setting forth the zero tolerance BAC limit for each state is set forth at Appendix 8.

In all states except Delaware, the established limit is an "illegal per se" violation—i.e., the driver's BAC is the determining factor to be considered in a prosecution for drunk driving.

New York's drunk driving statute contains a typical "illegal per se" provision relating to young drivers:

SECTION 1192-a. Operating a motor vehicle after having consumed alcohol; under the age of twenty-one; per se.

No person under the age of twenty-one shall operate a motor vehicle after having consumed alcohol as defined in this section. For purposes of this section, a person under the age of twenty-one is deemed to have consumed alcohol only if such person has .02 of one per centum or more . . . of alcohol in the person's blood, as shown by chemical analysis of such person's blood, breath, urine or saliva, made pursuant to the provisions of section eleven hundred ninety-four of this article.

License suspension or revocation, or some other statutorily prescribed penalty may result if the driver's BAC level tests at or above the reduced blood alcohol concentration levels. Early research from states where a zero tolerance policy has been implemented indicates it might reduce teenagers' nighttime fatal crashes.

In most states, a young driver is deemed to have given his or her consent to BAC testing. This is known as an "implied consent" provision. The Uniform Vehicle Code sets forth a typical implied consent provision concerning BAC testing of drivers under the age of 21:

SECTION 6-208(b). Any person under age (21) who drives or is in actual physical control of any vehicle upon the highways of this State shall be deemed to have given consent, subject to the provisions of § 11-903, to a test or tests of such person's blood, breath, or urine for the purpose of determining such person's alcohol concentration or the presence of other drugs . . .

The Uniform Vehicle Code further provides that, if the young driver either refuses to submit to the test, or tests at or above the established limit, his or her license will be revoked:

> SECTION 6-208(d). A person under age (21) requested to submit to a test as provided above shall be warned by the law enforcement officer requesting the test that a refusal to submit to the test will result in revocation of such person's license to operate a vehicle for (six months) (one year). Following this warning, if a person under arrest refuses upon the request of a law enforcement officer to submit to a test designated by the law enforcement agency as provided in paragraph (b) of this section, none shall be given.

> SECTION 6-208(e). If the person under the age (21) refuses testing or submits to a test which discloses an alcohol concentration of any measurable and detectable amount under this section, the law enforcement officer shall submit a sworn report to the department, certifying that the test was requested pursuant to subsection (b) and that the person refused to submit to testing or submitted to a test which disclosed an alcohol concentration of any measurable and detectable amount.

> SECTION 6-208(f). Upon receipt of the sworn report of a law enforcement officer submitted under subsection (e), the department shall revoke the driver's license of the person for the periods specified in § 6-214.

Graduated Licensing

Graduated licensing refers to the gradual advancement of a beginning young driver to an unrestricted driver. Under a graduated licensing system, the young driver is restricted from certain driving activities, such as driving at night or a limitation on passengers in the vehicle. In addition, special sanctions may be assessed to deter problems such as alcohol violations, speeding or other moving violations, and seat belt law violations. Those penalties may include an extension of the restricted driving period, or license suspension.

According to the model graduated licensing system developed by the National Committee on Uniform Traffic Laws and Ordinances (NCUTLO), violation of a state's "zero tolerance" law would prohibit a young driver from applying for an unrestricted license.

Presently, sixteen states have components of a graduated licensing system, including California, Colorado, Florida, Georgia, Kentucky, Illinois, Maryland, Massachusetts, Michigan, New Hampshire, New Jersey, New York, North Carolina, Pennsylvania, West Virginia, and Wisconsin. The National Highway Traffic Safety Administration rates each state's system against the NCUTLO model.

Adult Liability

If an child under the age of 21 drinks and drives, their parent or legal guardian may be liable if the child is responsible for causing damage, injury or death. If the adult purchased or provided the alcohol, his or her liability would be even greater. The consumption or possession of alcohol by the child would subject the adult to criminal prosecution and civil suit.

Most states recognize the right of a parent to serve their own underage children alcoholic beverages in the privacy of their home, however, they are not allowed to provide their children alcohol to be consumed elsewhere, nor are they permitted to serve alcohol to other underage children, even in their own home.

Nevertheless, according to a 1993 report by the Johnson Institute ("Johnson Report"), when school-age youth are allowed to drink alcohol at home, they are not only more likely to use alcohol and other drugs outside the home, they are more likely to develop serious behavioral and health problems related to their use of alcohol and other drugs. The Johnson Report also indicates that when parents "bargain" with their underage children— i.e., they allow them to drink as long as they promise not to drink and drive—they are more likely to drive after drinking or be in a vehicle driven by someone who has been drinking.

CHAPTER 6:

PENALTIES

In General

This chapter explores some of the penalties a drunk driver may suffer following a conviction. A thorough understanding of the range of penalties a jurisdiction may impose is imperative for an individual being prosecuted for drunk driving. Such penalties may include a fine; imprisonment; license suspension or revocation; and mandatory alcohol or drug abuse treatment. The reader is thus advised to consult his or her jurisdiction's statute for specific sentencing provisions.

License Suspension and Revocation

Whether or not a drunk driving defendant is sentenced to imprisonment, it is likely that his or her license will be suspended or revoked following conviction on a drunk driving offense. The majority of jurisdictions impose mandatory suspensions or revocations following a conviction for drunk driving. The severity of the penalty oftentimes depends on whether it was the driver's first offense or whether he or she is a repeat offender.

The Uniform Vehicle Code sets forth a typical license revocation provision:

SECTION 6-206. Mandatory revocation of license by department.

The department shall forthwith revoke the license of any driver upon receiving a record of such driver's conviction of any of the following offenses:

2. Driving or being in actual physical control of a motor vehicle while under the influence of alcohol or any drug as prohibited by § 11-902.

Administrative License Revocation (ALR) Laws

Among the most effective laws designed to deter drinking and driving are administrative license revocation (ALR) laws. An ALR law gives state officials the authority to administratively suspend the license of any driver who either fails a BAC test, or refuses to submit to the test. Because administrative licensing action is triggered by failing or refusing to take a chemical test—not by conviction—anyone arrested is immediately subject to suspension, and notice of the suspension is given to the driver immediately. Forty-one states and the District of Columbia have ALR laws.

A table of states with Administrative License Revocation (ALR) Laws is set forth at Appendix 12.

A temporary permit is usually issued to the driver, which may be valid for 7–45 days depending on the issuing state. During that time, the driver can appeal the suspension through administrative channels. However, if no appeal is filed, or if the appeal is not upheld, the license is suspended automatically for the prescribed period of time. Thus, ALR laws remove impaired drivers from the road quickly, and virtually ensure that penalties will be applied.

State laws vary in terms of blood alcohol concentration thresholds, length of time a temporary license is valid, the period within which a hearing must be held, and length of suspension. Suspensions may continue for 7 days to a year for first-time offenders, but most commonly last 90 days. Longer suspensions are specified for repeat violators. Extended periods of license suspension may be expected to have stronger deterrent effects, while those of short duration may have very limited effects. The National Highway Traffic Safety Administration (NHTSA) recommends that ALR laws impose at least a 90-day suspension or a 30-day suspension followed by 60 days of restricted driving.

A table of state administrative license suspension periods for first offenders is set forth at Appendix 13.

The success of laws against alcohol-impaired driving depends largely on deterrence, or keeping potential offenders off the roads in the first place. A well-publicized and enforced ALR law increases public perception that punishment for alcohol-impaired driving is likely to occur and will be swiftly applied and appropriately severe—a perception that is necessary to deter potential offenders. It is important to note that ALR laws do not replace criminal prosecution, which is handled separately through the courts.

Constitutional Considerations

Courts have held that although licenses are taken prior to a hearing, due process is provided because ALR laws allow for prompt post-suspension hearings. People whose licenses are suspended have the right to a prompt administrative hearing to determine the validity of the arrest and any alcohol testing.

Defendants have claimed that the double jeopardy clause of the U.S. Constitution prohibits the state from prosecuting an offender whose license has been suspended under an ALR statute. But high courts in several states have found that a criminal prosecution following ALR doesn't violate the double jeopardy clause.

Cost-Benefit Analysis

ALR laws are not costly to enforce. In most states, drivers who have their licenses suspended must pay a reinstatement fee to receive a new license at the end of the suspension period. These fees, which are paid by offenders and not taxpayers, can cover or exceed the cost of the program. In addition, states gained additional funds by qualifying for federal safety incentive grants.

An NHTSA study of three state programs found not only that direct revenues exceeded expenses, but also that state costs associated with nighttime crashes declined dramatically. A study conducted by the Insurance Institute for Highway Safety found that ALR laws reduce the number of drivers involved in fatal crashes by about 9 percent during the high-risk nighttime hours.

Restricted Licenses

Because license suspension is an extreme hardship on individuals who rely on driving as their primary means of making a livelihood, many states issue a restricted or conditional license, also known as a hardship license, that permits the offender to drive with a suspended license under limited circumstances, such as to and from work. States which permit driving during the license suspension period under certain conditions include Alaska, Arizona, Arkansas, California, Connecticut, District of Columbia, Florida, Georgia, Hawaii, Idaho, Illinois, Indiana, Iowa, Louisiana, Maine, Maryland, Minnesota, Nebraska, Nevada, New Mexico, New York, North Dakota, Ohio, Oklahoma, Oregon, Texas, West Virginia, Wisconsin, and Wyoming.

A table depicting restoration of driving privileges during suspension by state is set forth at Appendix 14.

Driver Alcohol Education Programs—First Time Offenders

Most states require a first time drunk driving offender to participate in an alcohol education program. A defendant may be able to work out a deal whereby his fine or license suspension period are reduced provided he successfully completes such a program.

A driver alcohol education program is designed to eliminate or reduce recidivism amongst drunk drivers; diagnose and recommend treatment; provide information about alcohol and/or drug abuse and increase awareness about the dangers of combining substance abuse and driving.

License Plate Sanctions

Many states have enacted laws which authorize the police to impound a drunk driver's license plates and revoke his or her registration, including Arizona, Arkansas, Delaware, Indiana, Kansas, Maine, Maryland, Michigan, Minnesota, New Hampshire, New York, North Dakota, Ohio, Oregon, Rhode Island, South Dakota, Virginia and Wyoming.

Under the Uniform Vehicle Code, conviction of the following offenses may result in license plate impoundment and registration revocation:

SECTION 17-301. Suspension of registration.

Upon conviction of any of the following offenses the court may, in addition to other penalties prescribed by this code, suspend the registration of any vehicle or vehicles registered in the name of the person convicted for a period of not to exceed [period of time] and any such suspension shall be immediately reported by the court to the department:

1. Homicide by vehicle (manslaughter resulting from the operation of a motor vehicle);

2. Driving or being in actual physical control of a motor vehicle while under the influence of alcohol or any drug;

3. Any felony in the commission of which a motor vehicle is used;

4. Failure to stop, render aid or identify oneself as required by § 10-102 in the event of a motor vehicle accident resulting in death or personal injury;

5. Unauthorized use of a motor vehicle belonging to another;

6. Driving while the privilege to do so is suspended or revoked;

7. Racing on a highway;

8. Willfully fleeing from or attempting to elude a police officer; or

9. Any offense punishable under § 17-201.

A table of states with vehicle license plate confiscation laws is set forth at Appendix 15.

Ignition Interlocks

Thirty-seven states have authorized either the discretionary or mandatory use of alcohol ignition interlock devices for drunk drivers. Ignition interlock devices analyze a driver's breath and disable the ignition if the driver has been drinking. Before starting the car, the driver must blow a sample of breath into the device. If the driver's blood alcohol concentration (BAC) level is below a specific limit, the engine will start. The car will not start if the BAC level exceeds the specified limit. Ignition interlock devices are generally intended for repeat and chronic drunk drivers, although they are authorized in some jurisdictions for first time offenders.

A table of states with laws requiring ignition interlock devices is set forth at Appendix 16.

Vehicle Immobilization

Some states have enacted laws which prevent an individual convicted of drunk driving from operating their vehicle by immobilizing it. This may be accomplished by placing a wheel lock—also known as a boot—on the car, or by installing a locking device on the steering wheel.

Vehicle Impoundment

When an individual is arrested on a drunk driving charge, his or her vehicle is generally impounded overnight. Ten states, including Florida, Indiana, Maryland, Minnesota, New York, North Dakota, Ohio, South Dakota, Utah, and Virginia, authorize vehicle impoundment for first time offenders as well as repeat offenders. Long-term impoundment of vehicles belonging to repeat drunk driving offenders is authorized in California, Delaware, Florida, Illinois, Iowa, Michigan, Missouri, Montana, Nebraska, Ohio, Oregon and Wisconsin.

Vehicle Forfeiture

In 21 states, including Alaska, Alabama, Arizona, Arkansas, California, Georgia, Maine, Minnesota, Missouri, Montana, New York, North Carolina, North Dakota, Ohio, Pennsylvania, Rhode Island, South Carolina, Tennessee, Texas, Washington and Wisconsin, repeat or multiple drunk driving offenders may forfeit vehicles that are driven while impaired by alcohol.

A table of states with vehicle forfeiture laws is set forth at Appendix 17.

In February 1999, New York City became the first jurisdiction to enact a law authorizing both the seizure and forfeiture of cars belonging to first-time drunk driving offenders. The policy is based on the city's forfeiture law, which allows police to seize any weapon used in a crime. It is intended to lower New York City's drunken-driving fatalities. Last year, 31 people were killed in the city as a result of drunken driving. New York City is the first to use a city forfeiture law to seize vehicles for drunk driving. In 23 other states, there are laws that allow police to confiscate or impound cars of drunken drivers, but they usually apply only to repeat offenders.

Under the New York law, a driver suspected of driving while intoxicated may be stopped and required to take a breath test. If the driver has a BAC level of 0.10 or higher, he will be arrested and his car seized. Drivers whose BAC is lower than 0.10 may be arrested for driving while impaired, but will not lose their car. Drivers who refuse to take the breath test can be charged with drunk driving and lose their cars based on the police officer's assessment of their behavior.

Once an arrest for drunk driving is made and the car is seized, there will follow both a criminal case against the drunk driver and a civil case seeking forfeiture of the vehicle. The New York Civil Liberties Union is testing the constitutionality of the new law on behalf of one of the first offenders to lose his car under the new crackdown.

Public Humiliation

Some jurisdictions have resorted to public humiliation as a means to deter drunk driving. For example, the drunk driver may be required to place an ad in the newspaper, a bumper sticker on his or her car, or wear a sign announcing their drunk driving behavior. The reasoning behind public humiliation is that since it is such a strong deterrent, it may make some offenders less likely to repeat the offense.

Public shaming has been used for several years in lower courts. Some federal courts are following the lead of lower courts and ordering guilty parties to announce their wrongdoing to the public through newspaper ads and bumper stickers. A district judge in Troy, Michigan has started ordering drunken drivers to attach bumper stickers to their cars that read: "Drunk Driving, you can't afford it." A Houston, Texas court sentenced a drunken driver to carry a sign outside a bar for five days announcing he killed two people while driving drunk.

Imprisonment

Sentencing structure among the states varies, thus, it would not be possible to set forth the penalties in detail in this almanac. Thus, the reader is advised to check the law of his or her jurisdiction for specific sentencing limitations. As an example, the Alabama sentencing statute for DWI offenders (Ala. Code § 32-5A-191) provides for a graduated increase in prison sentences depending on the number of offenses committed in a 5-year period:

First offense: Imprisonment for not more than 1 year . . .

Second offense within 5 years: Imprisonment, which may include hard labor, in a county or municipal jail for not more than 1 year . . .

Third offense within 5 years: 60 days (mandatory) to 1 year imprisonment, which may include hard labor, in county or municipal jail . . .

Fourth or subsequent offense within 5 years (Class C Felony): 1 year and 1 day (mandatory) to 10 years imprisonment, which may include hard labor for the county or state . . .

Some jurisdictions have adopted sentencing "guidelines" for a judge to follow, which establish a sentencing range based on certain aggravating and mitigating factors. Section 11-902 of the Uniform Vehicle Code sets forth the following penalties:

SECTION 11-902. Driving while under the influence of alcohol or drugs.

(c) In addition to the provisions of § 11-904, every person convicted of violating this section shall be punished by imprisonment for not less than 10 days or more than one year, or by fine of not less than $100 nor more than $1,000, or by both such fine and imprisonment and on a second or subsequent conviction, such person shall be punished by imprisonment for not less than 90 days nor more than one year, and, in the discretion of the court, a fine of not more than $1,000.

A table of states with mandatory imprisonment provisions for a first DWI conviction is set forth at Appendix 18.

In addition, many states which do not impose imprisonment on first-time offenders do require mandatory sentences of imprisonment for drivers convicted of second or subsequent drunk driving offenses. Harsher penalties are assessed if the driver is determined to be a "habitual offender," which may include commitment to a drug treatment facility.

For example, the Uniform Vehicle Code provides:

SECTION 11-904. Post-conviction examination and remedies.

(b) In addition to the penalties imposed by § 11-902(c), and after receiving the results of the examination in subsection (a) or, upon a hearing and determination that the person is an *habitual user* of alcohol or other drugs, the court may order supervised treatment on an outpatient basis, or upon additional determinations that the person constitutes a danger to self or others and that adequate treatment facilities are available, the court may order such person committed for treatment at a facility or institution approved by the (State Department of Health).

A table of states with mandatory imprisonment provisions for repeat DWI convictions is set forth at Appendix 19.

CHAPTER 7:

FEDERAL LEGISLATIVE PROGRAMS

In General

As set forth below, Congress has established a number of Federal programs designed to encourage states to enact effective drunk driving laws and prevention programs.

Incentive Grants under the Transportation Equity Act for the 21st Century (TEA-21)

On June 9, 1998, the President signed into law PL 105-178, the Transportation Equity Act for the 21st Century (TEA-21) authorizing highway, highway safety, transit and other surface transportation programs for the next 6 years. This new Act combines the continuation and improvement of current programs with new initiatives to meet the challenges of improving traffic safety. Significant features of TEA-21 relating to drunk driving include:

Incentives to Prevent Operation of Motor Vehicles by Intoxicated Persons

The Act provides $500 million for incentive grants for fiscal years 1998-2003 to states that have enacted and are enforcing a law providing that any person with a blood alcohol concentration of 0.08 percent or greater while operating a motor vehicle in the state shall be deemed to have committed a per se offense of driving while intoxicated.

Grants are based on the amount a state receives under the Section 402 Highway Safety program and may be used for any project eligible for assistance under Title 23 U.S.C.

Alcohol-impaired Driving Countermeasures

The Act revises the existing Section 410 alcohol-impaired driving countermeasures incentive grant program to deter drunk driving. Under this $219.5 million, 6-year program, the Secretary of Transportation will make basic grants to states that adopt and demonstrate specific programs, such as prompt suspension of the driver's license of an alcohol-impaired driver or graduated licensing systems for new drivers (Basic Grant A); or meet performance criteria showing reductions in fatalities involving impaired drivers (Basic Grant B). States receiving basic grants may be considered for up to six types of supplemental grants. States are eligible to receive grants for each of 6 fiscal years. The Section 410 alcohol-impaired driving counter-measures are further discussed below.

Highway Safety Research and Development

The Act continues the Section 403 Highway Safety Research and Development Program and specifies and allocates funds to a new category of research concerning measures that may deter drugged driving.

National Highway Traffic and Safety Administration Section 410 Program—Alcohol-Impaired Driving Countermeasures

The National Highway Traffic and Safety Administration (NHTSA) Section 410 program was originally established by Congress in 1988 and subsequently amended. Under the Section 410 program, states may qualify for basic and supplemental incentive grant funds by adopting and implementing comprehensive drunk driving prevention measures. To qualify for a grant under the 410 Program, a state is required to meet certain criteria.

Basic Grant Eligibility: Basic Grant A

A state shall become eligible for the Basic Grant A by adopting at least 5 of the following criteria:

1. Administrative License Revocation System—the establishment of an expedited administrative license suspension or revocation system for impaired drivers who either fail or refuse to take a chemical test, which results in a 90-day suspension for first time offenders, and either a 1-year suspension or revocation for repeat offenders.

2. Underage Drinking Program (Under Age 21)—establishment of an effective system for preventing individuals under age 21 from obtaining alcoholic beverages and for preventing persons from making alcoholic beverages available to individuals under age 21, including the issuance of "Under 21" driver's licenses that are tamper resistant or which are easily distinguishable in appearance from licenses issued to older drivers.

3. DWI Enforcement Program—establishment of either (i) a statewide program for stopping motor vehicles on a nondiscriminatory lawful basis for determining whether the driver is impaired, or (ii) a statewide special traffic enforcement program for impaired driving that emphasizes publicity for the program.

4. Graduated Licensing System—establishment of a 3-stage graduated licensing system for young drivers that includes nighttime driving restrictions during the first 2 stages, requires all vehicle occupants to be

properly restrained, and makes it unlawful for a person under age 21 to operate a motor vehicle with a BAC of 0.02 percent or greater.

5. Program for Drivers with High BAC Levels—establishment of a program to target individuals with high BAC levels who operate a motor vehicle, which may include implementation of a system of graduated penalties and assessment of individuals convicted of driving under the influence of alcohol.

6. Young Adult Drinking Program (Age 21-34)—establishment of a program to reduce driving while under the influence of alcohol by individuals age 21 through 34, which may include awareness campaigns, traffic safety partnerships, assessment of first-time offenders, and incorporating treatment into sentencing.

7. BAC Testing System—establishment of an effective system for increasing the rate of BAC testing of drivers involved in fatal accidents.

Basic Grant Eligibility: Basic Grant B

A state shall become eligible for the Basic Grant B by adopting the following criteria:

1. Fatal Impaired Driver Percentage Reduction—The state must demonstrate that the percentage of fatally injured drivers with 0.10 percent BAC or greater has decreased in each of the 3 most recent calendar years for which statistics for determining such percentages are available; and

2. Fatal Impaired Driver Percentage Comparison—The state must demonstrate that the percentage of fatally injured drivers with 0.10 percent BAC or greater has been lower than the average percentage for all states in each of the calendar years referred to above.

Supplemental Grants

Supplemental grants are available to states which meet 1 or more of the following criteria:

1. Video Equipment for Drunk Driver Detection Program—establishment of a program to acquire video equipment to be used in detecting and prosecuting drivers operating under the influence of alcohol.

2. Self-Sustaining Drunk Driving Prevention Program—establishment of a self-sustaining drunk driving prevention program under which a significant portion of the fines collected from individuals driving under the influence of alcohol are returned to those communities which have comprehensive DWI prevention programs.

3. Reduced Driving with Suspended License Law—establishment of a law aimed at reducing the incidence of individuals driving with suspended license, which may require a "zebra" stripe to be affixed and made clearly visible on the license plate of any motor vehicle owned and operated by a driver with a suspended license.

4. Use of Passive Alcohol Sensors—establishment of a program to acquire passive alcohol sensors to be used by law enforcement officers in detecting drivers operating under the influence of alcohol.

5. Effective DWI Tracking System—establishment of an effective DWI tracking system which may include data covering arrests, case prosecutions, court dispositions and sanctions.

6. Other Programs—establishment of other innovative programs to reduce traffic safety problems resulting from individuals driving while under the influence of alcohol or controlled substances, including programs that seek to achieve a reduction through legal, judicial, enforcement, educational, technological, or other approaches.

The IRS Restructuring Bill

In 1998, Congress passed legislation that requires states to (i) enact open container laws and (ii) provide for tougher penalties for repeat offenders. States that fail to comply with the legislation will have 1.5 percent of their federal highway construction funds funneled to traffic safety programs. States that do not pass the laws by October 1, 2003, will have 3 percent of their highway dollars redirected to safety programs.

Open Container Laws

The legislation requires all states to enact an open container law which prohibits the possession or consumption of an open container of alcohol by the driver and all passengers in a motor vehicle. Currently, only 27 states and the District of Columbia have some type of open container law, some of which only apply to the driver of the vehicle.

A table of states with open container laws is set forth at Appendix 20.

Repeat Offender Legislation

The legislation requires all states to establish stronger minimum penalties for repeat drunk-driving offenders, including: (i) a one-year minimum license suspension; (ii) vehicle impoundment provisions; (iii) vehicle immobilization or ignition interlock provisions; (iv) assessment and treatment of alcohol problems; and (v) mandatory jail time or community service for repeat offenders.

Failure to enact each of the required laws will result in the transfer of 1.5 percent of the state's Federal highway construction funds to its highway safety program for fiscal years 2001 and 2002 for states who fail to enact these laws by October 1, 2001 and 2002 respectively; and 3 percent for states that fail to enact legislation by October 1, 2003.

If funds are transferred to the state's highway safety program under this provision, the funds may be used for alcohol-impaired driving countermeasures, or may be directed to state and local agencies for enforcement of related laws.

This legislation was originally supposed to be included in the Transportation Equity Act for the 21st Century (TEA-21), however, it was omitted due to a technical error. Thus, the new laws were attached to the IRS Restructuring Bill.

The Federal Zero Tolerance Program

In November 1995, Congress established the Federal Zero Tolerance Program, which requires the withholding of certain Federal-aid highway funds from states that do not enact and enforce "zero tolerance" laws. To avoid withholding of funds, states were required to enact and enforce zero tolerance laws by October 1, 1998, that (i) set 0.02 percent BAC as the legal limit for all persons under the age of 21; (ii) make .0.2 percent BAC an "illegal per se" offense; and (iii) authorize license suspensions or revocations for any violation of the state zero tolerance law. As further set forth in Chapter 5, all states and the District of Columbia have since enacted zero tolerance laws.

Presidential Directive—The 0.08 BAC Percent Initiative

On March 3, 1998, President Clinton addressed representatives of national organizations, highway safety partners, and the nation, concerning proposed new federal standards to prevent impaired driving. The President called for a nationwide legal limit which would make it "illegal per se" to operate a motor vehicle at or above a BAC level of 0.08 percent across the country. The President directed the Secretary of Transportation to work with Congress, federal agencies, state governments, and other concerned groups to promote adoption of the limit, and consider the proposals listed below.

Public Education

The presidential directive proposes the development of an education campaign to help the public understand the risks associated with drinking and driving. Public education may include a broad range of activities such as high visibility enforcement campaigns, promotional events, and community-based initiatives. Supporting 0.08 percent BAC laws is a key part of any public health initiative to reduce the impaired driving problem.

Federal Lands

The presidential directive proposes setting the 0.08 percent BAC standard on Federal property, including national parks and Department of Defense installations.

The National Park Service (NPS)

Under 36 CFR Part 4, Subsection 4.23(a)(2) of the Vehicle and Traffic Regulations, the National Park Service (NPS) established a 0.10 percent per se legal limit for drivers who operate a vehicle on roadways or parking areas within all area parks open to public traffic that are under federal jurisdiction. The regulation further provides that if state law establishes more restrictive limits—e.g. a 0.08 percent BAC limit—those limits will supersede the federal limits.

Pursuant to President Clinton's March 3, 1998 directive, the NHTSA has worked with the NPS to promote the adoption of a national 0.08 percent BAC limit. In accordance with the presidential directive, the NPS has initiated plans to conduct rulemaking to amend its regulation to reduce the federal limit in its parks from 0.10 percent to 0.08 percent BAC limit.

Department of Defense (DOD) Installations

The Department of Defense (DOD) has jurisdiction over DOD Installations pursuant to 10 U.S.C. 113; 30112(g). Under this authority, the DOD has established a policy regarding drunk and drugged driving (Directive 101.7), which makes it illegal to operate a motor vehicle with a BAC of 0.10 percent or higher on a military installation or in areas where traffic operations are under military supervision. Operating a motor vehicle with a BAC of 0.10 percent or more is also a violation under the Uniform Code of Military Justice (UCMJ), 10 U.S.C. § 911.

Consequences of violating the BAC limit by DOD personnel are severe and may include loss of driving privileges, and disciplinary measures either by nonjudicial punishment or court martial. Punishments may include loss of pay, demotions, correctional custody and confinement.

Pursuant to the presidential directive, the NHTSA has worked with the DOD to promote the adoption of a national 0.08 percent BAC limit. In accordance with the presidential directive, the DOD has initiated plans to amend all applicable DOD directives and regulations to reduce the legal limit on DOD installations from 0.10 percent to 0.08 percent BAC limit, an action requiring Congressional approval.

Other Federal Property

A number of Federal agencies have jurisdiction over other types of Federal property. For example, the Bureau of Land Management (BLM), Department of the Interior (DOI), has jurisdiction over public lands in the United States, and the U.S. Forest Service (USFS), Department of Agriculture (USDA), has jurisdiction over National Forest System lands.

Pursuant to the presidential directive, the NHTSA has worked with the BLM and the USFS to determine whether a national .08 BAC legal limit should be adopted for the Federal properties they administer and over which they have Federal law enforcement jurisdiction.

Tribal Lands

The presidential directive proposes encouraging Tribal governments to adopt, enforce and publicize a 0.08 percent BAC standard on highways subject to their jurisdiction; and

Indian tribes, as domestic dependent sovereigns, possess the right of self-government, including the ability to enact their own laws relating to impaired driving and the responsibility for enforcing them. Pursuant to the Presidential directive dated March 3, 1998, NHTSA has worked with the Bureau of Indian Affairs (BIA), Department of the Interior (DOI), the Indian Health Service (IHS), and the Department of Health and Human Services, regarding the plans of these agencies to encourage the adoption of a .08 BAC legal limit on highways in tribal lands. In accordance with the directive, BIA and IHS plan to work with Indian tribes on a government-to-government basis to encourage the adoption, enforcement and publicity of a .08 BAC legal standard.

CHAPTER 8:

VICTIMS' RIGHTS

In General

When a family member is murdered, the survivors' only recourse is to resort to the criminal justice system to bring the criminal to justice, and thus provide the family with some closure to the tragedy. Historically, family members were not generally viewed as "victims of the crime," and they had little or no official involvement in the proceedings.

In recent years, this has begun to change, in large part due to the activism of the victims' rights movement. A victims rights movement has emerged over the past two decades to champion the rights of crime victims, including those victimized by the acts of drunk drivers. The victims' rights movement has fought to have the family of a homicide victim recognized as victims of the crime who are entitled to actively participate in the criminal proceedings. This movement has been responsible for the passage of important federal, state and local legislation that provide victims with certain rights and allow them to be active participants in the criminal justice process.

A common feature of many of these laws—sometimes referred to as a "Victims' Bill of Rights"—is the opportunity of victims to make their wishes known at the time of sentencing. This is known as a "victim impact statement," as further discussed below. Other statutory rights that may be provided to crime victims, witnesses to a crime, and the family members of a homicide victim include:

1. The right to attend the criminal proceedings, including the trial, the sentencing, and any subsequent parole hearings, and the right to be heard;

2. The right to be notified of each stage of the criminal proceedings so that the victim can participate if he or she wishes to do so.

3. The right to compensation—such as that provided by state victim compensation programs—and restitution by the offender, including the right to recover compensation derived from the criminal's exploitation of the crime;

4. The right to be informed of all available legal remedies, including the right to pursue civil action against the criminal, e.g. to recover punitive damages; and

5. The right to be protected from harassment, including security during the criminal proceedings, and relocation assistance if warranted;

6. The right to have the opportunity to inform the court of the impact of the crime and to request the court to submit such information to the parole board for inclusion in its records.

Under Section 11-1502 of the Uniform Vehicle Code, victims of a traffic-related offense are guaranteed the following rights:

Section 11-1502. Rights of Victims. Victims shall have the following rights:

(a) Speedy prosecution of the offense. In any criminal justice proceeding, the police, the prosecutor, and the court shall take appropriate action to ensure speedy prosecution of the defendant. Victims shall be informed by the prosecuting attorney of any motions which would result in delay of the prosecution and be allowed to object in writing.

(b) Upon request by the victim, to be informed by the police investigating the case of the status of the investigation, and by the prosecuting attorney prior to any critical decisions concerning the case including the charging decision, diversion, dismissal, or other disposition.

(c) To be present at any time the defendant has the right to be present during all criminal justice proceedings related to an offense unless the court determines that exclusion is necessary to protect the confidentiality of juvenile or similar proceedings. If a victim is unable to attend the court proceedings, the court may designate a representative of the victim who has the same right to be present as the victim would have had.

(d) To make victim impact statements to the court including information about the financial, emotional, psychological, and physical effects of the crime on the victim, the circumstances surrounding the crime, the manner in which it was perpetrated, and the victim's opinion of any recommended sentence of the convicted offender. A victim may present an impact statement to the court either orally or in writing.

(e) To an order of restitution if the order is authorized by the laws of the state.

As set forth in Appendix 6, the Uniform Vehicle Code also details the responsibilities incumbent upon the law enforcement agency and the prosecutor's office to provide victims of traffic-related offenses with resource information concerning support groups and the availability of services, and details about the criminal proceedings.

The Victim Impact Statement

A *victim impact statement* is a written or oral report which details the manner in which the crime affected the victim and the victim's family. The statement is commonly given at the time of sentencing, and at parole hearings at the time the criminal becomes eligible for parole.

The victim impact statement is usually offered by the victim, or the victim's survivors. In the case of a minor or incompetent victim, the statement may be offered by the parents or legal guardian of the victim.

The victim impact statement brings to the court's attention the pain and suffering caused by the crime, which may be expected to endure long after the criminal is sentenced. For example, the statement may describe the physical, mental or financial harm the crime has caused the family.

The victim impact statement also gives the victim and/or the victim's family, the chance to participate more fully in the criminal justice process and the quest to bring the criminal to justice. Many states even allow the victim to recommend a sentence or offer comments on the proposed sentence.

Most states have laws which give the victim and/or the victim's family, the right to make a victim impact statement, and require the court or the parole board to consider the statement when rendering a decision. The statement may also be contained in the criminal's presentencing report to the court, and periodically updated and sent to the parole board.

Under Section 11-1505 of the Uniform Vehicle Code, the Probation Department must include a written victim impact statement as part of the presentence report if the victim chooses to submit one:

> SECTION 11-1505. Probation Department. The Probation Department, in preparing any pre-sentence report on the defendant, must attempt to consult with the victim and must include a written victim impact statement as part of the pre-sentence report if the victim chooses to submit one. If the victim cannot be located or declines to cooperate, the probation officer must include a notation to that effect in the report.

In addition, Section 11-1506 of the Uniform Vehicle Code provides that the Court must orally inform victims present at the sentencing hearing of their right to present victim impact statements.

Victim Assistance Organizations

Crime victims often do not know where to turn for help in dealing with the emotional aftermath of the crime. Many local communities offer programs to assist the victim. Such programs are usually listed in the telephone directory under "victim's assistance." In addition, assistance may be found by contacting local social services or mental health organizations.

Most victims assistance organizations provide a wide variety of programs, including therapy and counseling; support groups; and practical help and information. For example, assistance may be provided in obtaining compensation from state victim compensation boards, or in completing a victim impact statement.

As further discussed below, one of the strongest advocates for those victimized by drunk drivers is Mothers Against Drunk Driving (MADD).

Mothers Against Drunk Driving (MADD)

Mothers Against Drunk Driving (MADD) is a non-profit grassroots organization begun by Cyndi Lightner, after her 13-year-old daughter, Cari, was killed by a hit-and-run drunk driver. The driver was a repeat offender and, prior to Cari's death, had been out of jail on bail for only two days after having caused another hit-and-run drunk driving crash. The driver also had three previous drunk driving arrests and two convictions. Cari's mother decided to take action so other families would not have to suffer the same tragedy.

MADD's stated mission is to look for effective solutions to drunk driving and underage drinking problems, and to assist victims of violent drunk driving crimes. MADD has been particularly effective in lobbying for victims' rights, and has initiated actions to bring about tougher laws against impaired driving, to provide for stiffer penalties for such crimes, and to increase greater public awareness on the perils of driving drunk.

Since its founding in 1980, MADD has helped pass more than 2,300 anti-drunk driving laws across the country. MADD has continued to grow and pursue the efforts initiated by its founder, and has approximately 600 chapters nationwide. MADD now has nearly three million members and supporters nationwide and abroad, making it the largest victim-advocate and anti-DWI activist organization in the USA and the world.

Along with its rapid growth, MADD recognized the need for more professional, trained management and administration and a more sophisticated approach to communications and dealing with the media, as well as training in DWI issues, the legislative process and victim assistance. Coordination to meet these needs is handled by a national headquarters staff of approximately 60 individuals who direct training opportunities, seasonal and ongoing education and awareness programs, national fundraising, media campaigns, and federal and state legislative activities.

Regular monthly or bimonthly mailings of program materials and other timely information from the National Office further reinforce the direction of the organization. Special training opportunities are held, including victim assistance institutes and impaired driving issues workshops, which may also include other pertinent state and community leaders outside of MADD. For more information, readers may contact MADD Headquarters at P.O. Box 541688, Dallas, TX 75354-1688.

APPENDICES

APPENDIX 1:

PERCENT OF FATALLY INJURED DRIVERS WITH BACS AT OR ABOVE 0.10 PERCENT, 1980–1997

YEAR	ALL DRIVERS	PASSENGER VEHICLE DRIVERS	TRACTOR-TRAILER DRIVERS	MOTORCYCLISTS
1980	51	54	15	46
1981	50	52	16	49
1982	49	50	16	47
1983	47	48	13	48
1984	44	45	14	45
1985	41	42	9	43
1986	41	42	4	43
1987	40	41	3	39
1988	40	41	7	39
1989	39	40	7	43
1990	41	41	10	43
1991	39	40	9	40
1992	37	38	6	39
1993	36	37	3	34
1994	35	36	4	32
1995	34	35	2	35
1996	33	33	3	34
1997	30	31	3	34

Source: Insurance Institute for Highway Safety.

APPENDIX 2:

TRAFFIC FATALITIES BY STATE—1997

STATE	TOTAL TRAFFIC FATALITIES	ALCOHOL-RELATED	PERCENT OF TOTAL
ALABAMA	1189	473	39.8%
ALASKA	77	41	52.8%
ARIZONA	951	433	45.5%
ARKANSAS	660	193	29.2%
CALIFORNIA	3688	1314	35.6%
COLORADO	613	218	35.6%
CONNECTICUT	338	152	45.0%
DELAWARE	143	61	42.7%
DISTRICT OF COLUMBIA	60	35	58.5%
FLORIDA	2782	934	33.6%
GEORGIA	1577	578	36.6%
HAWAII	131	59	44.7%
IDAHO	259	102	39.6%
ILLINOIS	1395	587	42.1%
INDIANA	935	308	32.9%
IOWA	468	174	37.2%
KANSAS	481	142	29.5%
KENTUCKY	857	279	32.6%
LOUISIANA	913	421	46.1%
MAINE	192	64	33.4%
MARYLAND	608	221	36.3%
MASSACHUSETTS	442	209	47.4%

STATE	TOTAL TRAFFIC FATALITIES	ALCOHOL-RELATED	PERCENT OF TOTAL
MICHIGAN	1446	558	38.6%
MINNESOTA	600	193	32.2%
MISSISSIPPI	861	344	40.0%
MISSOURI	1192	509	42.7%
MONTANA	265	120	45.3%
NEBRASKA	302	105	34.6%
NEVADA	347	160	46.2%
NEW HAMPSHIRE	125	60	47.7%
NEW JERSEY	774	282	36.4%
NEW MEXICO	484	220	45.5%
NEW YORK	1643	449	27.4%
NORTH CAROLINA	1483	528	35.6%
NORTH DAKOTA	105	50	47.8%
OHIO	1441	476	33.0%
OKLAHOMA	838	302	36.0%
OREGON	523	228	43.5%
PENNSYLVANIA	1557	631	40.5%
RHODE ISLAND	75	41	54.6%
SOUTH CAROLINA	903	318	35.2%
SOUTH DAKOTA	148	61	41.3%
TENNESSEE	1223	496	40.6%
TEXAS	3510	1748	49.8%
UTAH	366	75	20.6%
VERMONT	96	34	35.8%

STATE	TOTAL TRAFFIC FATALITIES	ALCOHOL-RELATED	PERCENT OF TOTAL
VIRGINIA	984	383	38.9%
WASHINGTON	676	300	44.4%
WEST VIRGINIA	379	146	38.6%
WISCONSIN	725	329	45.3%
WYOMING	137	43	31.5%
TOTAL	41,967	16,189	38.6%

Source: Mothers Against Drunk Driving.

APPENDIX 3:

PERCENT OF FATALLY INJURED PASSENGER VEHICLE DRIVERS WITH BACS AT OR ABOVE 0.10 PERCENT, BY GENDER AND AGE, 1997

AGE	MALE	FEMALE	ALL
16–20	32	13	26
21–30	51	22	43
31–40	52	33	46
41–50	43	21	36
51–60	28	10	22
OVER 60	10	3	8
ALL AGE GROUPS	37	17	31

Source: Insurance Institute for Highway Safety.

APPENDIX 4:

PERCENT OF FATALLY INJURED PASSENGER VEHICLE DRIVERS WITH BACS AT OR ABOVE 0.10 PERCENT, BY TIME OF DAY, 1997

TIME OF DAY	PERCENTAGE
Midnight–3:00 am	66
3:00 am–6:00 am	45
6:00 am–9:00 am	11
9:00 am–Noon	7
Noon–3:00 pm	11
3:00 pm–6:00 pm	18
6:00 pm–9:00 pm	33
9:00 pm–Midnight	52

Source: Insurance Institute for Highway Safety.

APPENDIX 5:

ALCOHOL-RELATED TRAFFIC FATALITIES—
HOLIDAY STATISTICS —1997

HOLIDAY	TOTAL TRAFFIC FATALITIES	TOTAL ALCOHOL-RELATED	PERCENTAGE ALCOHOL-RELATED	TIME PERIOD MONITORED
New Year's Eve/Day	192	129	67.1%	6pm 12/31/96– 5:59am 1/2/97
St. Patrick's Day	72	21	29.2%	6pm 3/17/97– 5:59am 3/18/97
Memorial Day	513	239	46.6%	6pm 5/23/97– 5:59am 5/27/97
Fourth of July	508	253	49.7%	6pm 7/3/97– 5:59am 7/7/97
Labor Day	507	254	50.1%	6pm 8/29/97– 5:59am 9/2/97
Halloween	138	54	39.0%	6pm 10/31/97– 5:59am 11/1/97
Thanksgiving	570	231	40.5%	6pm 11/26/97– 5:59am 12/2/97
Thanksgiving/ New Years	4058	1498	36.9%	6pm 11/27/97– 5:59am 12/31/97
Christmas	478	208	43.5%	6pm 12/24/97– 5:59am 2/29/97

Source: National Highway Transportation Safety Administration.

APPENDIX 6:

SELECTED PROVISIONS OF THE UNIFORM VEHICLE CODE RELATED TO DRUNK DRIVING

CHAPTER 6—ARTICLE I—ISSUANCE OF LICENSES, EXPIRATION AND RENEWAL

SECTION 6-103. Persons not to be licensed.

(b) Ineligibility. The department shall not issue any driver's license to, nor renew the driver's license of, any person:

1. Who is an habitual user of alcohol or any drug to a degree rendering such person incapable of safely driving a motor vehicle.

CHAPTER 6—ARTICLE I—CANCELLATION, SUSPENSION, OR REVOCATION OF LICENSES

SECTION 6-206. Mandatory revocation of license by department.

The department shall forthwith revoke the license of any driver upon receiving a record of such driver's conviction of any of the following offenses:

1. Homicide by vehicle (or manslaughter resulting from the operation of a motor vehicle;

2. Driving or being in actual physical control of a motor vehicle while under the influence of alcohol or any drug as prohibited by § 11-902;

3. Any felony in the commission of which a motor vehicle is used;

4. Failure to stop, render aid or identify the driver as required by § 10-102 in the event of a motor vehicle accident resulting in the death or personal injury of another;

5. Perjury or the making of a false affidavit or statement under oath to the department under this code or under any other law relating to the ownership or operation of motor vehicles.

6. Unauthorized use of a motor vehicle belonging to another which act does not amount to a felony;

7. The unlawful use of a license as prohibited by § 6-301(a).

SECTION 6-207. Revocation of license for refusal to submit to a chemical test or having BAC of 0.08 or more.

(a) Any person who operates a motor vehicle upon the highways of this State shall be deemed to have given consent, subject to the provisions of § 11-903, to a test or tests of such operator's blood, breath, or urine for the purpose of determining operator's alcohol concentration or the presence of other drugs. The test or tests shall be administered at the direction of a law enforcement officer who has probable cause to believe the person has been violating § 11-902(a), and one of the following conditions exists:

1. The person has been arrested for violating § 11-902(a) or any other offense alleged to have been committed while the person was violating § 11-902(a);

2. The person has been involved in an accident;

3. The person has refused to submit to the preliminary screening test authorized by § 6-209; or

4. The person has submitted to the preliminary screening test authorized by § 6-209 which disclosed an alcohol concentration of 0.08 or more.

The law enforcement agency by which such officer is employed shall designate which of the aforesaid tests shall be administered.

(b) Any person who is dead, unconscious or who is otherwise in a condition rendering one incapable of refusal, shall be deemed not to have withdrawn the consent provided by paragraph (a) of this section and the test or tests may be administered, subject to the provisions of § 11-903.

(c) A person requested to submit to a test as provided above shall be warned by the law enforcement officer requesting the test that a refusal to submit to the test will result in revocation of such person's license to operate a motor vehicle for (six months) (one year). Following this warning, if a person under arrest refuses upon the request of a law enforcement officer to submit to a test designated by the law enforcement agency as provided in paragraph (a) of this section, none shall be given.

(d) If the person refuses testing or submits to a test which discloses an alcohol concentration of 0.08 or more under this section, the law enforcement officer shall submit a sworn report to the department, certifying that the test was requested pursuant to subsection (a) and that the person refused to submit to testing or submitted to a test which disclosed an alcohol concentration of 0.08 or more.

(e) Upon receipt of the sworn report of a law enforcement officer submitted under subsection (d), the department shall revoke the driver's license of the person for the periods specified in § 6-214.

(f) On behalf of the department, the law enforcement officer submitting the sworn report under subsection (d) shall serve immediate notice of the revocation on the person, and the revocation shall be effective (7) (10) (15) days after the date of service. If the person has a valid license, the officer shall take the driver's license of the person, and issue a temporary license valid for the notice period. The officer shall send the license to the department along with the sworn report under subsection (d).

In cases where no notice has been served by the law enforcement officer, the department shall give notice as provided in § 2-314 and the revocation shall be effective (7) (10) (15) days after the date of service. If the address shown in the law enforcement officer's report differs from that shown on the department records, the notice shall be mailed to both addresses.

SECTION 6-208. Revocation of license for refusal to submit to chemical test or having BAC of any measurable and detectable amount for person under age (21).

(a) The phrase "any measurable and detectable amount of alcohol" shall be defined as the alcohol concentration in a person's blood or breath which is 0.02 or more based on the definition of blood and breath units as defined in § 11-903(a)(5).

(b) Any person under age (21) who drives or is in actual physical control of any vehicle upon the highways of this State shall be deemed to have given consent, subject to the provisions of § 11-903, to a test or tests of such person's blood, breath, or urine for the purpose of determining such person's alcohol concentration or the presence of other drugs. The test or tests shall be administered at the direction of a law enforcement officer who has probable cause to believe the person has been violating § 11-902 (a), and one of the following conditions exists:

1. The person under age (21) has been arrested for violating § 11-902 (a) or any other offense alleged to have been committed while the person was violating § 11-902 (a);

2. The person under age (21) has been involved in an accident;

3. The person under age (21) has refused to submit to the preliminary screening test authorized by § 6-209; or

4. The person under age (21) has submitted to the preliminary screening test authorized by § 6-209; which disclosed an alcohol concentration of any measurable and detectable amount.

The law enforcement agency by which such officer is employed shall designate which of the aforesaid tests shall be administered.

(c) Any person under age (21) who is dead, unconscious or who is otherwise in a condition rendering such person incapable of refusal, shall be deemed not to have withdrawn the consent provided by paragraph (b) of this section and the test or tests may be administered, subject to the provisions of § 11-903.

(d) A person under age (21) requested to submit to a test as provided above shall be warned by the law enforcement officer requesting the test that a refusal to submit to the test will result in revocation of such person's license to operate a vehicle for (six months) (one year). Following this warning, if a person under arrest refuses upon the request of a law enforcement officer to submit to a test designated by the law enforcement agency as provided in paragraph (b) of this section, none shall be given.

(e) If the person under the age (21) refuses testing or submits to a test which discloses an alcohol concentration of any measurable and detectable amount under this section, the law enforcement officer shall submit a sworn report to the department, certifying that the test was requested pursuant to subsection (b) and that the person refused to submit to testing or submitted to a test which disclosed an alcohol concentration of any measurable and detectable amount.

(f) Upon receipt of the sworn report of a law enforcement officer submitted under subsection (e), the department shall revoke the driver's license of the person for the periods specified in § 6-214.

(g) On behalf of the department, the law enforcement officer submitting the sworn report under subsection (e) shall serve immediate notice of the revocation on the person, and the revocation shall be effective (7) (10) (15) days after the date of service. If the person has a valid license, the officer shall take the driver's license of the person, and issue a temporary license valid for the notice period. The officer shall send the license to the department along with the sworn report under subsection (e).

In cases where no notice has been served by the law enforcement officer, the department shall give notice as provided in § 2-314 and the revocation shall be effective (7) (10) (15) days after the date of service. If the address shown in the law enforcement officer's report differs from that shown on the department records, the notice shall be mailed to both addresses.

SECTION 6-209. Preliminary breath test.

When a law enforcement officer has articulable grounds to suspect that a person may have been violating § 11-902(a), the officer may request the suspect to submit to a preliminary screening test of suspect's breath to determine such person's alcohol concentration using a device approved by the (State Department of Health) for that purpose. In addition to this test, or upon a refusal to submit to testing, the officer may require further testing under § 6-207.

SECTION 6-210. Chemical test of drivers in serious personal injury or fatal crashes.

Notwithstanding the provision's of § 6-207, when the driver of a vehicle is involved in an accident resulting in death or serious personal injury of another person, and there is reason to believe that the driver is guilty of a violation of § 11-902(a), the driver may be compelled by a police officer to submit to a test or tests of driver's blood, breath, or urine to determine the alcohol concentration or the presence of other drugs.

SECTION 6-211. Authority of department to suspend or revoke license.

(a) The department is hereby authorized to suspend the license of a driver upon a showing by its records or other sufficient evidence that the licensee:

1. Has committed an offense for which mandatory revocation of license is required upon conviction;

2. Has been convicted with such frequency of serious offenses against traffic regulations governing the movement of vehicles as to indicate a disrespect for traffic laws and a disregard for the safety of other persons on the highways;

3. Is an habitually reckless or negligent driver of a motor vehicle, such fact being established by the point system in subsection (b), by a record of accidents, or by other evidence;

4. Is incompetent to drive a motor vehicle;

5. Has permitted an unlawful or fraudulent use of such license;

6. Has violated driver's written promise to appear given to an officer upon the issuance of a traffic citation in this or any other state or has

failed to appear in court in this or any other state at the time specified by the court;

7. Has been convicted of fleeing or attempting to elude a police officer; or

8. Has been convicted of racing on the highways.

9. Has failed to comply with the compulsory insurance or financial responsibility requirements of Chapter 7, where license suspension is specifically authorized under that chapter.

(b) For the purpose of identifying habitually reckless or negligent drivers and habitual or frequent violators of traffic regulations governing the movement of vehicles, the department shall adopt regulations establishing a uniform system assigning demerit points for convictions of violations of Chapter 11 of this code or of ordinances adopted by local authorities regulating the operation of motor vehicles. The regulations shall include a designated level of point accumulation which so identifies drivers. The department may assess points for convictions in other states of offenses which, if committed in this State, would be grounds for such assessment. Notice of each assessment of points may be given, but notice is required when the point accumulation reaches (xx) percent of the number at which suspension is authorized. No points shall be assessed for violating a provision of this code or municipal ordinance regulating standing, parking, equipment, size or weight. In case of the conviction of a licensee of two or more traffic violations committed on a single occasion, such licensee shall be assessed points for one offense only and if the offenses involved have different point values, such licensee shall be assessed for the offense having the greater point value. The department is authorized to suspend the license of a driver when such person's driving record identifies driver as an habitually reckless or negligent driver or as an habitual or frequent violator under this subsection. The department may, in accordance with its rules and regulations, order the licensee to attend a group or private driver improvement interview regarding such person's driving ability and record.

SECTION 6-212. Opportunity for hearing required.

(a) A suspension or revocation of a license under § 6-114, 6-211, or 10-109 shall not become effective until the person is notified in writing and given an opportunity for a hearing.

1. The hearing shall be held within 20 days after receipt of a request for a hearing in the county where the alleged offense occurred unless the

department and the licensee agree to a hearing in some other county. A record of all hearings shall be made.

2. Upon such hearing, the department shall rescind its order of revocation or suspension or, good cause appearing therefor, may modify or reaffirm its order.

(b) A revocation of license under Section § -207 shall become effective (7) (10) (15) days after the date of service of the notice of revocation.

1. At any time prior to the hearing provided in subsection (b)2, the person may request in writing an administrative review of the order of revocation. Upon receiving the request the department shall review the order, the evidence upon which it is based, including whether the person was driving or in actual physical control of a motor vehicle, and any other material information brought to the attention of the department, and determine whether sufficient cause exists to sustain the order. Within 15 days of receiving the request, the department shall report in writing the results of the review. The availability of the administrative review of the order shall have no effect upon the availability of judicial review as provided in § 6-219.

2. Any person whose license is revoked under § 6-207 may request a hearing in writing. The request shall state the grounds upon which the person seeks to have the revocation rescinded. The filing of the request shall not stay the revocation. The hearing shall be held within 20 days after filing of the request in the county in which the alleged offense occurred, unless the person and the department agree to a different location. The hearing shall be recorded, and be conducted by the department's designated agent. The hearing may be conducted upon a review of the law enforcement officer's own reports; provided, however, that the person may subpoena the officer. The department may issue subpoenas to compel the attendance of witnesses.

The scope of the hearing shall be limited to the issues of:

(1) Whether the law enforcement officer requested the test pursuant to § 6-207;

(2) Whether the person was warned as required by § 6-207(c);

(3) Whether the person was driving or in actual physical control of a motor vehicle;

(4) Whether the person refused to submit to the testing as provided in § 6-207; or

(5) Whether a properly administered test or tests disclosed an alcohol concentration of 0.08 or more.

SECTION 6-214. Period of revocation.

(a) Unless the revocation was for a cause which has been removed, any person whose license or privilege to drive a motor vehicle on the public highways has been revoked shall not be eligible to apply for a new license nor restoration of such person's nonresident operating privilege until the expiration of:

1. (Six months) (One year) from the date on which the revoked license was surrendered to and received by the department or from such other date as shall be determined by the department in cases of revocation for; refusal to submit to a chemical test under the provisions of § 6-207. (REVISED, 1984.)

2. (Three months) (Six months) from the date on which the revoked license was surrendered to and received by the department or from such other date as shall be determined by the department in cases of revocation for submitting to a test disclosing an alcohol concentration of 0.08 or more under the provisions of § 6-207.

3. One year from the date on which the license was surrendered to a court under § 6-205.

4. One year from the date on which the revoked license was surrendered to and received by the department.

5. Or, in all other revocation cases, one year commencing on a date determined by the department.

(b) Following a license revocation under § 6-206(2) or 6-207, the department shall not issue a new license or otherwise restore the driving privilege unless and until the person presents evidence satisfactory to the department that it will be reasonably safe to permit the person to drive a motor vehicle upon the highways. No driving privilege may be restored until all applicable reinstatement fees have been paid.

(c) Except for revocations under § 6-206(2) and 6-207, the department shall not issue a new license nor restore a person's revoked nonresident operating privilege unless and until it is satisfied after investigation of the character, habits and driving ability of such person that it will be safe to grant the privilege of driving a motor vehicle on the highways.

(d) Where a license or driving privilege has been revoked under § 6-207 and the person is also convicted on criminal charges arising out of the same event for a violation of an offense under § 11-902(a), and a revocation has been imposed under § 6-206(2), both revocations shall be imposed but the total period of revocation shall not exceed the longer of the two revocation periods.

SECTION 6-215. Limited license.

Notwithstanding § 6-214 and 6-303, following a license revocation under § 6-206(2) or 6-207, the department may issue after 30 days a limited license to the driver if no prior limited license has been issued within the preceding 12 months and there have been no other such prior revocations. The department in issuing a limited license may impose the conditions and limitations which in its judgment are necessary to the interests of the public safety and welfare. The license may be limited to the operation of particular vehicles and to particular classes and time of operation. The limited license issued by the department shall clearly indicate the limitations imposed and the driver operating under a limited license shall have the license in driver's possession at all times when operating as a driver.

SECTION 6-216. Period of suspension.

(a) The department shall not suspend a driver's license or privilege to drive a motor vehicle on the public highways for a period of more than one year, except as permitted under § 6-303 or under Chapter 7.

(b) At the end of the period of suspension a license surrendered to the department under § 6-217 shall be returned to the licensee.

SECTION 6-217. Surrender and return of license; duty of officers.

(a) The department upon canceling, suspending or revoking a license shall require that such license shall be surrendered to and be retained by the department.

(b) Any person whose license has been canceled, suspended or revoked shall immediately return the license to the department.

(c) A law enforcement officer who in the course of duty encounters any canceled, suspended, or revoked drivers license shall seize and return such license to the department immediately.

SECTION 6-218. No operation under foreign license during suspension or revocation in this State.

Any resident or nonresident whose driver's license or privilege to operate a motor vehicle in this State has been suspended or revoked as provided in this code shall not operate a motor vehicle in this State under a license or permit issued by any other jurisdiction or otherwise during such suspension or after such revocation until a new license is obtained when and as permitted under this chapter.

SECTION 6-219. Right of appeal to court.

(a) Any person denied a license or whose license has been canceled or revoked by the department, except where such cancellation or revocation is mandatory under the provisions of this code, and except any person whose license has been revoked under § 6-207 shall have the right to file a petition within 30 days thereafter for a hearing in the matter in (a court of record) in the county wherein such person shall reside, or in the case of a nonresident's operating privilege in the county in which the main office of the department is located, and such court is hereby vested with jurisdiction and it shall be its duty to set the matter for hearing upon 30 days' written notice to the department, and thereupon to take testimony and examine into the facts of the case and to determine whether the petitioner is entitled to a license or is subject to denial, cancellation or revocation of license under the provisions of this chapter.

(b) Any person whose driving privileges have been revoked under the provisions of § 6-207, may petition the (court of record) in the county in which such person resides for review of the decision on administrative review conducted under § 6-212. The petition for review shall state the factual and legal claims upon which the petitioner relies, and shall be filed within (15) (30) days after notice of the decision on administrative review, together with proof of service of a copy thereof upon the department. The court shall set the matter for review upon thirty days' written notice to the department upon receipt of the record. The review shall be on the record, without taking additional testimony. If the court finds that the department exceeded its constitutional or statutory authority, made an erroneous interpretation of the law, acted in an arbitrary and capricious manner, or made a determination which is unsupported by the evidence in the record, the court may reverse the department's determination.

Filing the petition for appeal shall not stay the revocation.

Any person whose license has been suspended is entitled to judicial review under (cite law comparable to § 15 of the Model State Administrative Procedure Act).

CHAPTER 6—ARTICLE III—
VIOLATION OF LICENSE PROVISIONS

SECTION 6-303. Driving while license suspended or revoked.

(a) Any person who drives a motor vehicle on any highway of this State at a time when such person's privilege to do so is suspended or revoked shall be guilty of a misdemeanor and upon conviction shall be punished by imprisonment for not less than two days nor more than six months and there may be imposed in addition thereto a fine of not more than $500.

(b) Upon receiving a record of conviction of any driver for violating subsection (a) or any law or ordinance regulating the operation of motor vehicles where the offense was committed at a time when such person's license was suspended or revoked, the department may extend the period of suspension or revocation for an additional period of one year from and after the date upon which the period of suspension or revocation would otherwise have terminated.

CHAPTER 6—ARTICLE V—
COMMERCIAL DRIVER'S LICENSE ACT

SECTION 6-514. Disqualification and cancellation.

(a) Disqualification Offenses. Any person is disqualified from driving a commercial motor vehicle for a period of not less than one year if convicted of a first violation of:

1. Driving or being in the actual physical control of a commercial motor vehicle under the influence of alcohol; or

2. Driving or being in the actual physical control of a commercial motor vehicle under the influence of any other drug or combination of other drugs to a degree which render the person incapable of safely driving; or

3. Driving or being in the actual physical control of a commercial motor vehicle under the combined influence of alcohol and any other drug or drugs to a degree which renders the person incapable of safely driving; or

4. Driving or being in the actual physical control of a commercial motor vehicle while the alcohol concentration of the person's blood or breath is 0.04 or more as defined by this code: or

5. Leaving the scene of an accident when that person is driving a commercial motor vehicle; or

6. Using a commercial motor vehicle in the commission of any felony; or

7. Refusal to submit to a test or tests to determine the driver's alcohol concentration or presence of other drugs while driving a commercial motor vehicle. If any of the above violations occur while transporting a hazardous material required to be placarded, the person shall be disqualified for a period of not less than three years.

(b) A person is disqualified for life for a second conviction of any of the offenses specified in paragraph (a), or any combination of those offenses, arising from 2 or more separate incidents.

(c) The department may issue regulations establishing guidelines, including conditions, under which a disqualification for life under paragraph (b) may be reduced to a period of not less than ten years.

(d) A person is disqualified from driving a commercial motor vehicle for life who uses a commercial motor vehicle in the commission of any felony involving the manufacture, distribution, or dispensing of a controlled substance, or possession with intent to manufacture, distribute or dispense a controlled substance.

(e) A person is disqualified from driving a commercial motor vehicle for a period of not less than 60 days if convicted of 2 serious traffic violations, committed in a commercial motor vehicle, arising from separate incidents, occurring within a 3-year period. However, a person will be disqualified from driving a commercial motor vehicle for a period of not less than 120 days if convicted of 3 serious traffic violations, committed in a commercial motor vehicle arising from separate incidents, occurring within a 3-year period.

(f) After suspending, revoking, or canceling a commercial driver license, the department shall update the driver's records to reflect that action within 10 days. After suspending or revoking the driving privilege of any person who has been issued a CDL or commercial driver instruction permit from another jurisdiction, the department shall notify the licensing authority of the state which issued the CDL or commercial driver instruction permit within 10 days.

SECTION 6-516. Prohibited alcohol offenses for commercial motor vehicle drivers.

(a) Notwithstanding any other provisions of this code, a person shall not drive a commercial motor vehicle within this state while having any measurable or detectable amount of alcohol in such person's system.

(b) A person who drives a commercial motor vehicle within this state while having any measurable or detectable amount of alcohol in such person's system, or who refuses to submit to an alcohol test under § 6-517 of this Chapter, must be placed out of service for 24 hours.

(c) Any person who drives a commercial motor vehicle within this state with an alcohol concentration of 0.04 or more shall, in addition to any other sanctions which may be imposed under this code, be disqualified from driving a commercial motor vehicle under § 6-514 of this Chapter.

SECTION 6-517. Implied consent requirements for commercial motor vehicle drivers.

(a) A person who drives a commercial motor vehicle within this state is deemed to have given consent, subject to administrative procedures established in this code, to take a test or tests of that person's blood, breath or urine for the purpose of determining that person's alcohol concentration or the presence of other drugs.

(b) A test or tests may be administered at the direction of a law enforcement officer, who after stopping or detaining the commercial motor vehicle driver, has probable cause to believe that driver was driving a commercial motor vehicle while having alcohol or drugs in such driver's system.

(c) A person requested to submit to a test or tests as provided in Subsection (a) above must be warned by the law enforcement officer requesting the test or tests, that a refusal to submit to the test or tests will result in that person being immediately placed out-of-service for a period of 24 hours and may result in being disqualified from operating a commercial motor vehicle for a period of not less than 12 months.

(d) If the person refuses testing, or submits to a test which discloses alcohol concentration of 0.04 or more, the law enforcement officer must submit a sworn report to the department certifying that the test was requested pursuant to Subsection (a) and that the person refused to submit to testing, or submitted to a test which disclosed an alcohol concentration of 0.04 or more.

(e) Upon receipt of the sworn report of a law enforcement officer submitted under Subsection (d), the department must disqualify the driver from driving a commercial motor vehicle under § 6-514 of this Chapter.

SECTION 6-518. Notification of traffic convictions.

Within ten days after receiving a report of the conviction of any non-resident holder of a commercial driver license for any violation of state law or local ordinance relating to motor vehicle traffic control, other than parking violations, committed in a commercial motor vehicle, the department must notify the driver licensing authority in the licensing state of the conviction.

CHAPTER 10—ACCIDENTS AND ACCIDENT REPORTS

SECTION 10-102-Accidents involving death or personal injury

(a) The driver of any vehicle involved in an accident resulting in injury to or death of any person shall immediately stop such vehicle at the scene of such accident or as close thereto as possible but shall then forthwith return to and in every event shall remain at the scene of the accident until such driver has fulfilled the requirements of § 10-104. Every such stop shall be made without obstructing traffic more than is necessary.

(b) Any person failing to stop or to comply with said requirements under such circumstances shall, upon conviction, be punished by imprisonment for not less than 30 days nor more than one year or by fine of not less than $100 nor more than $5,000 or by both such fine and imprisonment.

SECTION 10-104. Duty to give information and render aid.

(a) The driver of any vehicle involved in an accident resulting in injury to or death of any person or damage to any vehicle or other property which is driven or attended by any person shall give the driver's name, address and the registration number and owner of the vehicle the driver is operating and shall upon request and if available exhibit such driver's license or permit to drive to any person injured in such accident or to the driver or occupant of or person attending any vehicle or other property damaged in such accident and shall give such information and upon request exhibit such license or permit to any police officer at the scene of the accident or who is investigating the accident and shall render to any person injured in such accident reasonable assistance, including the carrying, or the making of arrangements for the carrying, of such person to a physician, surgeon, or hospital for medical or surgical treatment if it is apparent that such treatment is necessary, or if such carrying is requested by the injured person.

(b) In the event that none of the persons specified are in condition to receive the information to which they otherwise would be entitled under subdivision (a) of this section, and no police officer is present, the driver of any vehicle involved in such accident after fulfilling all other requirements of § 10-102 and subdivision (a) of this section, insofar as possible on his or her part to be performed, shall forthwith report such accident to the nearest office of a duly authorized police authority and submit thereto the information specified in subdivision (a) of this section.

SECTION 10-116. Chemical tests in fatal crashes.

(a) When an accident results in the death of any driver or pedestrian within four hours of the accident, the medical examiner (or official performing like functions) shall withdraw blood or another bodily substance from the deceased driver or pedestrian so the amount of alcohol or the presence of other drugs in such person's blood can be determined. When possible, the withdrawal shall occur within eight hours of death.

(b) Subsection (a) shall not require withdrawing blood or any other bodily substance from a pedestrian who was less than 16 years of age at the time of such person's death.

(c) The medical examiner (or official performing like functions) or an approved laboratory shall analyze the blood or other substance to determine the amount of alcohol or the presence of other drugs in the dead driver's or pedestrian's blood.

(d) The results of the analysis required by this section shall be reported to the department and may be used by state and local officials only for statistical purposes that do not reveal the identity of the deceased person. Nothing in this subsection shall restrict the tests as evidence in criminal or civil proceedings.

(e) Withdrawal of blood or another bodily substance and its analysis shall comply with requirements of the (State Department of Health).

CHAPTER 11—ARTICLE IX—SERIOUS TRAFFIC OFFENSES

SECTION 11-902. Driving while under the influence of alcohol or drugs.

(a) A person shall not drive or be in actual physical control of any vehicle while:

1. The alcohol concentration in such person's blood or breath is 0.08 or more based on the definition of blood and breath units in § 11-903(a) (5);

OPTIONAL I. The alcohol concentration in such person's blood or breath as measured within three hours of the time of driving or being in the actual physical control is 0.08 or more based on the definition of blood and breath units in § 11-903. If proven by a preponderance of evidence, it shall be an affirmative defense to a violation of this subsection that the defendant consumed a sufficient quantity of alcohol after the time of driving or actual physical control of a vehicle and before the administration of the evidentiary test to cause the defendant's alcohol concentration to be 0.08 or more. The foregoing provision shall not limit the introduction of any other competent evidence bearing upon the question whether or not the person violated this section, including tests obtained more than three hours after such alleged violation.

2. Under the influence of alcohol;

3. Under the influence of any other drug or combination of other drugs to a degree which renders such person incapable of safely driving; or

4. Under the combined influence of alcohol and any other drug or drugs to a degree which renders such person incapable of safely driving.

(b) The fact that any person charged with violating this section is or has been legally entitled to use alcohol or other drug shall not constitute a defense against any charge of violating this section.

(c) In addition to the provisions of § 11-904, every person convicted of violating this section shall be punished by imprisonment for not less than 10 days or more than one year, or by fine of not less than $100 nor more than $1,000, or by both such fine and imprisonment and on a second or subsequent conviction, such person shall be punished by imprisonment for not less than 90 days nor more than one year, and, in the discretion of the court, a fine of not more than $1,000.

SECTION 11-903. Chemical and other test.

(a) Upon the trial of any civil or criminal action or proceeding arising out of acts alleged to have been committed by any person while driving or in actual physical control of a vehicle while under the influence of alcohol or other drugs, evidence of the concentration of alcohol or other drugs in a person's blood or breath at the time alleged, as determined by analysis of the person's blood, urine, breath or other bodily substance, shall be admissible, Where such a test is made the following provisions shall apply:

1. Chemical analyses of the person's blood, urine, breath, or other bodily substance to be considered valid under the provisions of this section shall have been performed according to methods approved by the (State Department of Health) and by an individual possessing a valid permit issued by the (State Department of Health) for this purpose. The (State Department of Health) is authorized to approve satisfactory techniques or methods, to ascertain the qualifications and competence of individuals to conduct such analyses, and to issue permits which shall be subject to termination or revocation at the discretion of the (State Department of Health).

2. When a person shall submit to a blood test at the request of a law enforcement officer under the provisions of § 6-207 or 6-210, only a physician or a registered nurse (or other qualified person) may withdraw blood for the purpose of determining the alcoholic or other drug content therein. This limitation shall not apply to the taking of breath or urine specimens.

3. The person tested may have a physician, or a qualified technician, chemist, registered nurse, or other qualified person of such person's own choosing administer a chemical test or tests in addition to any administered at the direction of a law enforcement officer. The failure or inability to obtain an additional test by a person shall not preclude the admission of evidence relating to the test or tests taken at the direction of a law enforcement officer.

4. Upon the request of the person who shall submit to a chemical test or tests at the request of a law enforcement officer, full information concerning the test or tests shall be made available to the person or such person's attorney.

5. Alcohol concentration shall mean either grams of alcohol per 100 milliliters of blood or grams of alcohol per 2l0 liters of breath.

(b) Upon the trial of any civil or criminal action or proceeding arising out of acts alleged to have been committed by any person while driving or in actual physical control of a vehicle while under the influence of alcohol, the concentration of alcohol in the person's blood or breath at the time alleged as shown by analysis of the person's blood, urine, breath, or other bodily substance shall give rise to the following presumptions:

1. If there was at that time an alcohol concentration less than 0.08, such fact shall not give rise to any presumption that the person was or was not under the influence of alcohol, but such fact may be considered with other competent evidence in determining whether the person was under the influence of alcohol.

2. If there was at that time an alcohol concentration of 0.08 or more, it shall be presumed that the person was under the influence of alcohol.

3. The foregoing provisions of this subsection shall not be construed as limiting the introduction of any other competent evidence bearing upon the question whether the person was under the influence of alcohol.

(c) If a person under arrest refuses to submit to a chemical test under the provisions of § 6-207, evidence of refusal shall be admissible in any civil or criminal action or proceeding arising out of acts alleged to have been committed while the person was driving or in actual physical control of a motor vehicle while under the influence of alcohol or other drugs.

SECTION 11-904. Post conviction examination and remedies.

(a) Before sentencing any person convicted of violating § 11-902, the court shall conduct or order an appropriate examination or examinations to determine whether the person needs or would benefit from treatment for alcohol or other drug abuse.

(b) In addition to the penalties imposed by § 11-902(c), and after receiving the results of the examination in subsection (a) or, upon a hearing and determination that the person is an habitual user of alcohol or other drugs, the court may order supervised treatment on an outpatient basis, or upon additional determinations that the person constitutes a danger to self or others and that adequate treatment facilities are available, the court may order such person committed for treatment at a facility or institution approved by the (State Department of Health).

(c) Any person subject to this section may be examined by a physician of such person's own choosing and the results of any such examination shall be considered by the court.

(d) No commitment or supervised treatment on an outpatient basis ordered under subsection (b) shall exceed one year. Upon motion duly made by the convicted person, an attorney, a relative or an attending physician, the court at any time after an order of commitment shall review said order. After determining the progress of treatment, the court may order its continuation or the court may order the person's release, supervised treatment on an out-patient basis, or it may impose penalties specified by this code giving credit for the time of commitment.

(e) Upon application by any person under an order of commitment or supervised treatment for a driver's license, the results of the examination referred to in subsection (a) and a report of the progress of the treatment ordered shall be forwarded by the applicant to the department for consideration by the health advisory board (appointed under § 6-119).

(f) The department may after receiving the advice of the health advisory board issue a license to such person with conditions and restrictions consistent with the person's rehabilitation and with protection of the public notwithstanding the provisions of § 6-214.

SECTION 11-905. Limits on Plea Bargaining.

When the prosecution agrees to a plea of guilty or nolo contendere to a charge of a violation other than § 11-902(a) in satisfaction of, or as a substitute for, an original charge of a violation of § 11-902(a), the prosecution shall state for the record a factual basis for the satisfaction, or substitution, including whether or not there had been consumption of any alcoholic beverage or ingestion or administration of any other drug, or both, by the defendant in connection with the offense.

SECTION 11-906. Homicide by vehicle.

(a) Whoever shall unlawfully and unintentionally cause the death of another person while engaged in the violation of any state law or municipal ordinance applying to the operation or use of a vehicle or to the regulation of traffic shall be guilty of homicide when such violation is the proximate cause of said death.

(b) Any person convicted of homicide by vehicle shall be fined not less than $500 nor more than $2,000, or shall be imprisoned in the county jail not less than three months nor more than one year, or may be so fined and so imprisoned, or shall be imprisoned in the penitentiary for a term not less than one year nor more than five years.

ARTICLE XII—OPERATION OF BICYCLES, OTHER HUMAN-POWERED VEHICLES, AND MOPEDS

SECTION 11-1202. Traffic laws apply to persons on bicycles and other human powered vehicles.

Every person propelling a vehicle by human power or riding a bicycle shall have all of the rights and all of the duties applicable to the driver of any other vehicle under Chapters 10 and 11, except as to special regulation sin this article and except as to those provisions which by their nature can have no application.

ARTICLE XIII—SPECIAL RULES FOR MOTORCYCLES

SECTION 11-1301. Traffic laws apply to persons operating motorcycles.

Every person operating a motorcycle shall be granted all of the rights and shall be subject to all of the duties applicable to the driver of any other vehicle under this code, except as to special regulations in this article and except as to those provisions of this code which by their nature can have no application.

ARTICLE XV—VICTIMS OF A TRAFFIC-RELATED OFFENSE

SECTION 11-1502. Rights of victims.

Victims shall have the following rights:

(a) To speedy prosecution of the offense. In any criminal justice proceeding, the police, the prosecutor, and the court shall take appropriate action to ensure speedy prosecution of the defendant. Victims shall be informed by the prosecuting attorney of any motions which would result in delay of the prosecution and be allowed to object in writing.

(b) Upon request by the victim, to be informed by the police investigating the case of the status of the investigation, and by the prosecuting attorney prior to any critical decisions concerning the case including the charging decision, diversion, dismissal, or other disposition.

(c) To be present at any time the defendant has the right to be present during all criminal justice proceedings related to an offense unless the court determines that exclusion is necessary to protect the confidentiality of juvenile or similar proceedings. If a victim is unable to attend the court proceedings, the court may designate a representative of the victim who has the same right to be present as the victim would have had.

(d) To make victim impact statements to the court including information about the financial, emotional, psychological, and physical effects of the crime on the victim, the circumstances surrounding the crime, the manner in which it was perpetrated, and the victim's opinion of any recommended sentence of the convicted offender. A victim may present an impact statement to the court either orally or in writing.

(e) To an order of restitution if the order is authorized by the laws of this state.

SECTION 11-1503. Law Enforcement Agency.

(a) At the time of the initial contact between any law enforcement agency and the victim, the law enforcement agency investigating the case shall provide the victim a written statement of rights which shall include the following information:

1. A statement and explanation of the victim's rights as enumerated by § 11-1502 of this code;

2. The availability of victim assistance, medical and emergency services;

3. The availability of victim compensation benefits, including the name, office address, and telephone number of the contact person(s) responsible for administering the program; and

4. The office addresses and telephone numbers of appropriate victim support and services groups.

(b) As soon as available, the police shall provide to the victim the following:

1. The office address and telephone number of the prosecutor's office;

2. The case number and the names, office addresses, and telephone numbers of the law enforcement officers assigned to investigate the case; and

3. If known, whether the suspect has been taken into custody, and if taken into custody, whether released, and any conditions attached to the release.

SECTION 11-1504. Prosecutor.

(a) Upon request by the victim for information concerning the criminal court proceedings, a prosecuting attorney shall inform the victim of the following:

1. A statement and explanation of the victim's rights as enumerated by § 11-1502;

2. The actual assignment of the case, including case number, and the court to which it is assigned;

3. The date, time, and location of any criminal proceedings relative to the offense;

4. The availability of crime victim compensation benefits, including the name, office address, and telephone numbers of contact persons responsible for administering the program;

5. The availability of any transportation services to court proceedings;

6. Whether the defendant has a right to review the pre-sentence reports and impact statements;

7. Whether the defendant has the right to attend and make a statement at the sentencing hearing;

8. The time and place of any hearing for the reconsideration of the sentence imposed; and

9. The right to receive information from corrections officials concerning imprisonment and release.

10. If the defendant appeals, the prosecutor shall inform the victim of the status of the case on appeal and the decision of the appellate court upon disposition.

(b) The prosecutor shall notify the victim in writing of the date, time, and location of the sentencing hearing and advise the victim of the opportunity to present a victim's impact statement or to appear at the sentencing proceeding.

SECTION 11-1505. Probation Department.

The Probation Department, in preparing any pre-sentence report on the defendant, must attempt to consult with the victim and must include a written victim impact statement as part of the pre-sentence report if the victim chooses to submit one. If the victim cannot be located or declines to cooperate, the probation officer must include a notation to that effect in the report.

SECTION 11-1506. Court.

The Court shall orally inform victims present at the sentencing hearing of their right to present victim impact statements.

CHAPTER 16—ARTICLE I—PARTIES TO CRIME, OWNERS, AND PUBLIC EMPLOYEES

SECTION 16-101. Parties to a crime.

Every person who commits, attempts to commit, conspires to commit, or aids or abets in the commission of, any act declared in this code to be a crime, whether individually or in connection with one or more other persons or as a principal, agent or accessory, shall be guilty of such offense, and every person who falsely, fraudulently, forcibly or willfully induces, causes, coerces, requires, permits or directs another to violate any provision of this code is likewise guilty of such offense.

16-102. Offenses by persons owning or controlling vehicles.

It is unlawful for the owner, or any other person, employing or otherwise directing the driver of any vehicle to require or knowingly to permit the operation of such vehicle upon a highway in any manner contrary to law.

SECTION 16-103. Public officers and employees-exceptions

The provisions of chapters 10, 11, 12, 13 and 14 applicable to drivers of vehicles upon the highways shall apply to the drivers of all vehicles owned or operated by the United States, this State or any county, city, town, district or any other political subdivision of the State, subject to such specific exceptions as are set forth in this code.

ARTICLE II—ARRESTS AND ISSUANCE OF CITATIONS

SECTION 16-201. Procedure upon arrest for felony.

Whenever a person is arrested for any violation of this code declared herein to be a felony, such person shall be dealt with in like manner as upon arrest for the commission of any other felony. For the purposes of this section any offense which may be punishable by imprisonment in a state penitentiary is a felony.

SECTION 16-202. Arrests for serious offenses.

(a) The authority of a police officer to make an arrest is the same as upon an arrest for a felony when such officer has reasonable and probable grounds to believe that the person arrested has committed any of the following offenses:

1. Homicide by vehicle;

2. Driving or being in actual physical control of a vehicle while under the influence of alcohol or any drug as prohibited by § 11-902.

3. Failure to stop, or failure to give information, or failure to render reasonable assistance, in the event of an accident resulting in death or personal injuries, as prescribed in § 10-102 and 10-104.

4. Failure to stop, or failure to give information, in the event of an accident resulting in damage to a vehicle or to other property, as prescribed in § 10-103 to 10-105 inclusive;

5. Reckless driving;

6. Racing on the highway; or

7. Willfully fleeing from or attempting to elude a police officer. Provided, however, that the manner of making arrests under this section shall be as in misdemeanor cases.

(b) Whenever any person is arrested as authorized in this section such person shall be taken without unnecessary delay before the proper magistrate as specified in § 10-208, except that in the case of the offenses designated in paragraphs 4, 5, 6 and 7, a police officer shall have the same discretion as is provided in other cases in § 16-204.

CHAPTER 17—ARTICLE II—FELONIES

SECTION 17-201. Penalty for felony.

Any person who is convicted of a violation of any of the provisions of this code herein or by the laws of this State declared to constitute a felony shall be punished by imprisonment for not less than one year nor more than five years, or by a fine of not less than $500 nor more than $5,000, or by both such fine and imprisonment.

ARTICLE III—REGISTRATION

SECTION 17-301. Suspension of registration.

Upon conviction of any of the following offenses the court may, in addition to other penalties prescribed by this code, suspend the registration of any vehicle or vehicles registered in the name of the person convicted for a period of not to exceed [period of time] and any such suspension shall be immediately reported by the court to the department:

1. Homicide by vehicle (manslaughter resulting from the operation of a motor vehicle);

2. Driving or being in actual physical control of a motor vehicle while under the influence of alcohol or any drug;

3. Any felony in the commission of which a motor vehicle is used;

4. Failure to stop, render aid or identify oneself as required by § 10-102 in the event of a motor vehicle accident resulting in death or personal injury;

5. Unauthorized use of a motor vehicle belonging to another;

6. Driving while the privilege to do so is suspended or revoked;

7. Racing on a highway;

8. Willfully fleeing from or attempting to elude a police officer; or

9. Any offense punishable under § 17-201.

APPENDIX 7:

STATE ILLEGAL PER SE BLOOD ALCOHOL CONCENTRATION (BAC) LEVELS—ALL DRIVERS

STATE	ILLEGAL PER SE BAC LEVEL
ALABAMA	0.08
ALASKA	0.10
ARIZONA	0.10
ARKANSAS	0.10
CALIFORNIA	0.08
COLORADO	0.10
CONNECTICUT	0.10
DELAWARE	0.10
DISTRICT OF COLUMBIA	0.10
FLORIDA	0.08
GEORGIA	0.10
HAWAII	0.08
IDAHO	0.08
ILLINOIS	0.08
INDIANA	0.10
IOWA	0.10
KANSAS	0.08
KENTUCKY	0.10

STATE	ILLEGAL PER SE BAC LEVEL
LOUISIANA	0.10
MAINE	0.08
MARYLAND	0.10
MASSACHUSETTS	NONE*
MICHIGAN	0.10
MINNESOTA	0.10
MISSISSIPPI	0.10
MISSOURI	0.10
MONTANA	0.10
NEBRASKA	0.10
NEVADA	0.10
NEW HAMPSHIRE	0.08
NEW JERSEY	0.10
NEW MEXICO	0.08
NEW YORK	0.10
NORTH CAROLINA	0.08
NORTH DAKOTA	0.10
OHIO	0.10
OKLAHOMA	0.10
OREGON	0.08
PENNSYLVANIA	0.10

STATE	ILLEGAL PER SE BAC LEVEL
RHODE ISLAND	0.10
SOUTH CAROLINA	NONE*
SOUTH DAKOTA	0.10
TENNESSEE	0.10
TEXAS	0.10
UTAH	0.08
VERMONT	0.08
VIRGINIA	0.08
WASHINGTON	0.08
WEST VIRGINIA	0.10
WISCONSIN	0.10
WYOMING	0.10

*Laws in Massachusetts and South Carolina are not per se laws. A BAC of 0.10 percent in South Carolina and 0.08 percent in Massachusetts is evidence of alcohol impairment but is not illegal per se.

Source: Insurance Institute for Highway Safety.

APPENDIX 8:

STATE ILLEGAL PER SE BLOOD ALCOHOL CONCENTRATION (BAC) LEVELS—YOUNG DRIVERS (UNDER 21)

STATE	ILLEGAL PER SE BAC LEVEL
ALABAMA	.02
ALASKA	.00
ARIZONA	.00
ARKANSAS	.02
CALIFORNIA	.01
COLORADO	.02
CONNECTICUT	.02
DELAWARE	.02*
DISTRICT OF COLUMBIA	.02
FLORIDA	.02
GEORGIA	.02
HAWAII	.02
IDAHO	.02
ILLINOIS	.00
INDIANA	.02
IOWA	.02
KANSAS	.02
KENTUCKY	.02

STATE	ILLEGAL PER SE BAC LEVEL
LOUISIANA	.02
MAINE	.00
MARYLAND	.02
MASSACHUSETTS	.02
MICHIGAN	.02
MINNESOTA	.00
MISSISSIPPI	.08
MISSOURI	.02
MONTANA	.02
NEBRASKA	.02
NEVADA	.02
NEW HAMPSHIRE	.02
NEW JERSEY	.01
NEW MEXICO	.02
NEW YORK	.02
NORTH CAROLINA	.00
NORTH DAKOTA	.02
OHIO	.02
OKLAHOMA	.00
OREGON	.00
PENNSYLVANIA	.02

STATE	ILLEGAL PER SE BAC LEVEL
RHODE ISLAND	.02
SOUTH CAROLINA	N/A
SOUTH DAKOTA	N/A
TENNESSEE	.02
TEXAS	.00
UTAH	.00
VERMONT	.02
VIRGINIA	.02
WASHINGTON	.02
WEST VIRGINIA	.02
WISCONSIN	.02**
WYOMING	N/A

*In Delaware the .02 percent BAC law for young drivers is not a per se law.
**The Wisconsin statute applies to drivers under the age of 19.
Source: Insurance Institute for Highway Safety.

APPENDIX 9:

STATES WITH MANDATORY BLOOD ALCOHOL CONCENTRATION (BAC) LEVEL TESTING

STATE	MANDATORY TESTING
ALABAMA	NO
ALASKA	YES
ARIZONA	NO
ARKANSAS	YES
CALIFORNIA	YES
COLORADO	YES
CONNECTICUT	YES
DELAWARE	YES
DISTRICT OF COLUMBIA	YES
FLORIDA	YES
GEORGIA	NO
HAWAII	YES
IDAHO	YES
ILLINOIS	YES
INDIANA	YES
IOWA	YES
KANSAS	YES
KENTUCKY	YES

STATE	MANDATORY TESTING
LOUISIANA	YES
MAINE	YES
MARYLAND	YES
MASSACHUSETTS	NO
MICHIGAN	YES
MINNESOTA	YES
MISSISSIPPI	YES
MISSOURI	YES
MONTANA	NO
NEBRASKA	YES
NEVADA	YES
NEW HAMPSHIRE	NO
NEW JERSEY	YES
NEW MEXICO	YES
NEW YORK	YES
NORTH CAROLINA	YES
NORTH DAKOTA	YES
OHIO	NO
OKLAHOMA	YES
OREGON	NO
PENNSYLVANIA	NO
RHODE ISLAND	NO
SOUTH CAROLINA	NO
SOUTH DAKOTA	YES
TENNESSEE	NO
TEXAS	YES
UTAH	YES

STATE	MANDATORY TESTING
VERMONT	NO
VIRGINIA	NO
WASHINGTON	YES
WEST VIRGINIA	NO
WISCONSIN	YES
WYOMING	YES

Source: Mothers Against Drunk Driving (MADD).

APPENDIX 10:

STATES WITH SOBRIETY CHECKPOINTS

STATE	SOBRIETY CHECKPOINTS
ALABAMA	YES
ALASKA	NO RULING
ARIZONA	YES
ARKANSAS	YES
CALIFORNIA	YES
COLORADO	YES
CONNECTICUT	YES
DELAWARE	YES
DISTRICT OF COLUMBIA	YES
FLORIDA	YES
GEORGIA	YES
HAWAII	YES
IDAHO	NO
ILLINOIS	YES
INDIANA	YES
IOWA	YES
KANSAS	YES
KENTUCKY	YES
LOUISIANA	NO

STATE	SOBRIETY CHECKPOINTS
MAINE	YES
MARYLAND	YES
MASSACHUSETTS	YES
MICHIGAN	NO
MINNESOTA	NO
MISSISSIPPI	YES
MISSOURI	YES
MONTANA	YES
NEBRASKA	YES
NEVADA	NO RULING
NEW HAMPSHIRE	YES
NEW JERSEY	YES
NEW MEXICO	YES
NEW YORK	YES
NORTH CAROLINA	NO
NORTH DAKOTA	YES
OHIO	YES
OKLAHOMA	YES
OREGON	NO
PENNSYLVANIA	YES
RHODE ISLAND	NO

STATE	SOBRIETY CHECKPOINTS
SOUTH CAROLINA	YES
SOUTH DAKOTA	YES
TENNESSEE	YES
TEXAS	NO
UTAH	YES
VERMONT	YES
VIRGINIA	YES
WASHINGTON	NO
WEST VIRGINIA	YES
WISCONSIN	NO
WYOMING	NO

Source: Mothers Against Drunk Driving (MADD).

NHTSA/ANACAPA SFST VALIDATION DATA FORM

Officer ID:_____   Driver: ☐ Adult   ☐ Male
                                 ☐ Under 21   ☐ Female
                                 ↳ Age:_____

Month____ Day____ 1996 Time of Stop:_____ hr _____ min

FIELD SOBRIETY TESTS ADMINISTERED ☑

1.   HORIZONTAL GAZE NYSTAGMUS TEST ☐

	Clues	
	Right Eye	Left Eye
Lack of smooth pursuit	☐	☐
Nystagmus at maximum deviation	☐	☐
Nystagmus onset before 45 degrees	☐	☐
Clues	☐ +	☐ =

Total HGN Clues (6 clues maximum) ☐ ←
4 or more ≥ 0.08 / 2 or more ≥ 0.04

2.   ONE LEG STAND TEST ☐ (seconds)

	Clues		
	0-10	11-20	21-30
Sways while balancing			
Uses arms for balance			
Hops to maintain balance			
Puts foot down			
Cannot perform test (4 clues – maximum)			
Total One Leg Stand Clues			

2 or more ≥ 0.08

3.   WALK AND TURN TEST ☐

	Clues
Loses balance while listening to instructions	☐
Starts before instructions are finished	☐

	1st 9	2nd 9
Stops while walking		
Does not touch heel to toe		
Steps off the line		
Raises arms for balance		
Incorrect number of steps		
Trouble with turn (explain)_____		
Cannot perform the test (8 clues – maximum)		
Total Walk and Turn Clues		

2 or more ≥ 0.08

4.   ESTIMATE OF BAC BASED ON SFSTs: [ ]

Time of estimation _____ hr _____ min

5.   SUBJECT BAC   ☐ Refused

PBT→ [ ]   Time of PBT test _____ hr _____ min

Other→ [ ]   Time of other test _____ hr _____ min

→ ☐ Breath   ☐ Blood   ☐ Urine

6.   DISPOSITION: ☐ Warning   ☐ Citation   ☐ DUI Arrest

Figure 3. Data collection form used in the validation study.

APPENDIX 12:

STATES WITH ADMINISTRATIVE LICENSE
REVOCATION (ALR) LAWS

Alabama

Alaska

Arizona

Arkansas

California

Colorado

Connecticut

Delaware

District of Columbia

Florida

Georgia

Hawaii

Idaho

Illinois

Indiana

Iowa

Kansas

Louisiana

Maine

Maryland

Massachussetts

Minnesota

Mississippi

Missouri

Nebraska

Nevada

New Hampshire

New Mexico

North Carolina

North Dakota

Ohio

Oklahoma

Oregon

Texas

Utah

Vermont

Virginia

West Virginia

Wisconsin

Wyoming

Source: Mothers Against Drunk Driving (MADD)

APPENDIX 13:

STATE ADMINISTRATIVE LICENSE SUSPENSION PERIODS—1ST OFFENSE

STATE	SUSPENSION PERIOD
ALABAMA	90 DAYS
ALASKA	90 DAYS
ARIZONA	90 DAYS
ARKANSAS	120 DAYS
CALIFORNIA	4 MONTHS
COLORADO	3 MONTHS
CONNECTICUT	90 DAYS
DELAWARE	3 MONTHS*
DISTRICT OF COLUMBIA	2-90 DAYS
FLORIDA	6 MONTHS*
GEORGIA	1 YEAR
HAWAII	3 MONTHS
IDAHO	90 DAYS
ILLINOIS	3 MONTHS
INDIANA	180 DAYS*
IOWA	180 DAYS*
KANSAS	30 DAYS*
KENTUCKY	N/A
LOUISIANA	90 DAYS
MAINE	90 DAYS*
MARYLAND	45 DAYS*
MASSACHUSETTS	90 DAYS

STATE	SUSPENSION PERIOD
MICHIGAN	N/A
MINNESOTA	90 DAYS*
MISSISSIPPI	90 DAYS
MISSOURI	30 DAYS
MONTANA	N/A*
NEBRASKA	90 DAYS
NEVADA	90 DAYS
NEW HAMPSHIRE	6 MONTHS*
NEW JERSEY	N/A
NEW MEXICO	90 DAYS
NEW YORK	VARIABLE**
NORTH CAROLINA	10 DAYS
NORTH DAKOTA	91 DAYS*
OHIO	90 DAYS*
OKLAHOMA	180 DAYS
OREGON	90 DAYS*
PENNSYLVANIA	N/A
RHODE ISLAND	N/A
SOUTH CAROLINA	N/A
SOUTH DAKOTA	N/A*
TENNESSEE	N/A
TEXAS	60 DAYS
UTAH	90 DAYS*
VERMONT	90 DAYS
VIRGINIA	7 DAYS*

STATE	SUSPENSION PERIOD
WASHINGTON	90 DAYS
WEST VIRGINIA	6 MONTHS
WISCONSIN	6 MONTHS
WYOMING	90 DAYS*

* An offender's vehicle may be impounded or immobilized, the registration may be suspended, or the license tags may be confiscated. In New York, registration suspension applies only to offenders younger than 21. In Montana, impoundment applies only to offenders younger than 18.

** In New York, administrative license suspension lasts until prosecution is complete.

Source: Insurance Institute for Highway Safety.

APPENDIX 14:

RESTORATION OF DRIVING PRIVILEGES DURING SUSPENSION PERIOD BY STATE

STATE	RESTORATION OF PRIVILEGES	CONDITIONS
ALABAMA	NO	
ALASKA	YES	AFTER 30 DAYS
ARIZONA	YES	AFTER 30 DAYS
ARKANSAS	YES	
CALIFORNIA	YES	AFTER 30 DAYS*
COLORADO	NO	
CONNECTICUT	YES	
DELAWARE	NO	
DISTRICT OF COLUMBIA	YES	
FLORIDA	YES	
GEORGIA	YES	
HAWAII	YES	AFTER 30 DAYS
IDAHO	YES	AFTER 30 DAYS
ILLINOIS	YES	AFTER 30 DAYS
INDIANA	YES	AFTER 30 DAYS
IOWA	YES	
KANSAS	NO	
KENTUCKY	N/A	
LOUISIANA	YES	AFTER 30 DAYS
MAINE	YES	
MARYLAND	YES	
MASSACHUSETTS	NO	

STATE	RESTORATION OF PRIVILEGES	CONDITIONS
MICHIGAN	N/A	
MINNESOTA	YES	AFTER 15 DAYS
MISSISSIPPI	NO	
MISSOURI	NO	
MONTANA	N/A	
NEBRASKA	YES	AFTER 30 DAYS
NEVADA	YES	AFTER 45 DAYS
NEW HAMPSHIRE	NO	
NEW JERSEY	N/A	
NEW MEXICO	YES	AFTER 30 DAYS,
NEW YORK	YES	
NORTH CAROLINA	NO	
NORTH DAKOTA	YES	AFTER 30 DAYS
OHIO	YES	AFTER 15 DAYS
OKLAHOMA	YES	
OREGON	YES	AFTER 30 DAYS
PENNSYLVANIA	N/A	
RHODE ISLAND	N/A	
SOUTH CAROLINA	N/A	
SOUTH DAKOTA	N/A	
TENNESSEE	N/A	
TEXAS	YES	
UTAH	NO	
VERMONT	NO	
VIRGINIA	NO	

STATE	RESTORATION OF PRIVILEGES	CONDITIONS
WASHINGTON	YES	AFTER 30 DAYS
WEST VIRGINIA	YES	AFTER 30 DAYS
WISCONSIN	YES	
WYOMING	YES	

*Drivers usually must demonstrate special hardship to justify restoring privileges during suspension, and then privileges often are restricted.

Source: Insurance Institute for Highway Safety.

APPENDIX 15:

STATES WITH VEHICLE LICENSE PLATE
CONFISCATION LAWS

STATE	LICENSE PLATE CONFISCATION
ALABAMA	NO
ALASKA	NO
ARIZONA	YES
ARKANSAS	NO
CALIFORNIA	NO
COLORADO	NO
CONNECTICUT	NO
DELAWARE	NO
DISTRICT OF COLUMBIA	NO
FLORIDA	NO
GEORGIA	NO
HAWAII	NO
IDAHO	NO
ILLINOIS	NO
INDIANA	YES
IOWA	YES
KANSAS	NO
KENTUCKY	NO
LOUISIANA	NO

STATE	LICENSE PLATE CONFISCATION
MAINE	YES
MARYLAND	NO
MASSACHUSETTS	NO
MICHIGAN	NO
MINNESOTA	YES
MISSISSIPPI	NO
MISSOURI	NO
MONTANA	NO
NEBRASKA	NO
NEVADA	NO
NEW HAMPSHIRE	YES
NEW JERSEY	NO
NEW MEXICO	NO
NEW YORK	YES
NORTH CAROLINA	NO
NORTH DAKOTA	YES
OHIO	YES
OKLAHOMA	NO
OREGON	YES
PENNSYLVANIA	NO
RHODE ISLAND	YES

STATE	LICENSE PLATE CONFISCATION
SOUTH CAROLINA	NO
SOUTH DAKOTA	YES
TENNESSEE	NO
TEXAS	NO
UTAH	NO
VERMONT	NO
VIRGINIA	YES
WASHINGTON	NO
WEST VIRGINIA	NO
WISCONSIN	NO
WYOMING	YES

Source: Mothers Against Drunk Driving (MADD).

APPENDIX 16:

STATES WITH LAWS REQUIRING IGNITION INTERLOCK DEVICES

STATE	IGNITION INTERLOCK LAW
ALABAMA	NO
ALASKA	YES
ARIZONA	YES
ARKANSAS	YES
CALIFORNIA	YES
COLORADO	YES
CONNECTICUT	NO
DELAWARE	YES
DISTRICT OF COLUMBIA	NO
FLORIDA	YES
GEORGIA	YES
HAWAII	YES
IDAHO	YES
ILLINOIS	YES
INDIANA	YES
IOWA	YES
KANSAS	YES
KENTUCKY	NO
LOUISIANA	YES

STATE	IGNITION INTERLOCK LAW
MAINE	YES
MARYLAND	YES
MASSACHUSETTS	NO
MICHIGAN	YES
MINNESOTA	NO
MISSISSIPPI	NO
MISSOURI	YES
MONTANA	YES
NEBRASKA	YES
NEVADA	YES
NEW HAMPSHIRE	NO
NEW JERSEY	NO
NEW MEXICO	YES
NEW YORK	YES
NORTH CAROLINA	YES
NORTH DAKOTA	YES
OHIO	YES
OKLAHOMA	YES
OREGON	YES
PENNSYLVANIA	NO
RHODE ISLAND	YES

STATE	IGNITION INTERLOCK LAW
SOUTH CAROLINA	NO
SOUTH DAKOTA	NO
TENNESSEE	YES
TEXAS	YES
UTAH	YES
VERMONT	NO
VIRGINIA	YES
WASHINGTON	YES
WEST VIRGINIA	YES
WISCONSIN	YES
WYOMING	NO

Source: Insurance Institute for Highway Safety.

APPENDIX 17:

STATES WITH VEHICLE FORFEITURE LAWS

STATE	VEHICLE FORFEITURE
ALABAMA	NO
ALASKA	YES
ARIZONA	YES
ARKANSAS	YES
CALIFORNIA	YES
COLORADO	NO
CONNECTICUT	NO
DELAWARE	NO
DISTRICT OF COLUMBIA	NO
FLORIDA	NO
GEORGIA	YES
HAWAII	NO
IDAHO	NO
ILLINOIS	NO
INDIANA	NO
IOWA	NO
KANSAS	NO
KENTUCKY	NO
LOUISIANA	YES

STATE	VEHICLE FORFEITURE
MAINE	YES
MARYLAND	NO
MASSACHUSETTS	NO
MICHIGAN	NO
MINNESOTA	YES
MISSISSIPPI	YES
MISSOURI	NO
MONTANA	YES
NEBRASKA	NO
NEVADA	NO
NEW HAMPSHIRE	NO
NEW JERSEY	NO
NEW MEXICO	NO
NEW YORK	YES
NORTH CAROLINA	YES
NORTH DAKOTA	YES
OHIO	YES
OKLAHOMA	NO
OREGON	NO
PENNSYLVANIA	YES
RHODE ISLAND	YES

STATE	VEHICLE FORFEITURE
SOUTH CAROLINA	YES
SOUTH DAKOTA	NO
TENNESSEE	YES
TEXAS	YES
UTAH	NO
VERMONT	YES
VIRGINIA	NO
WASHINGTON	YES
WEST VIRGINIA	NO
WISCONSIN	YES
WYOMING	NO

Source: Insurance Institute for Highway Safety.

STATES WITH MANDATORY IMPRISONMENT FOR
FIRST DWI CONVICTION

STATE	MANDATORY IMPRISONMENT
ALABAMA	NO
ALASKA	YES
ARIZONA	NO
ARKANSAS	NO
CALIFORNIA	NO
COLORADO	YES*
CONNECTICUT	YES
DELAWARE	NO
DISTRICT OF COLUMBIA	NO
FLORIDA	NO
GEORGIA	YES
HAWAII	YES
IDAHO	NO
ILLINOIS	NO
INDIANA	NO
IOWA	YES
KANSAS	YES
KENTUCKY	YES
LOUISIANA	YES

STATE	MANDATORY IMPRISONMENT
MAINE	YES
MARYLAND	NO
MASSACHUSETTS	NO
MICHIGAN	NO
MINNESOTA	NO
MISSISSIPPI	NO
MISSOURI	NO
MONTANA	YES**
NEBRASKA	NO
NEVADA	NO
NEW HAMPSHIRE	NO
NEW JERSEY	NO
NEW MEXICO	NO
NEW YORK	NO
NORTH CAROLINA	NO
NORTH DAKOTA	NO
OHIO	NO
OKLAHOMA	NO
OREGON	YES
PENNSYLVANIA	YES
RHODE ISLAND	NO

STATE	MANDATORY IMPRISONMENT
SOUTH CAROLINA	YES
SOUTH DAKOTA	NO
TENNESSEE	YES
TEXAS	NO
UTAH	YES
VERMONT	NO
VIRGINIA	NO
WASHINGTON	YES
WEST VIRGINIA	YES
WISCONSIN	NO
WYOMING	NO

*Applies only to first illegal per se conviction.

**This sanction only applies to driving while under the influence offense.

APPENDIX 19:

STATES WITH MANDATORY IMPRISONMENT FOR REPEAT DWI OFFENSES

STATE	MANDATORY IMPRISONMENT
ALABAMA	YES
ALASKA	YES
ARIZONA	YES
ARKANSAS	YES
CALIFORNIA	YES
COLORADO	YES
CONNECTICUT	YES
DELAWARE	YES*
DISTRICT OF COLUMBIA	NO
FLORIDA	YES
GEORGIA	YES
HAWAII	YES
IDAHO	YES
ILLINOIS	YES
INDIANA	YES
IOWA	YES
KANSAS	YES
KENTUCKY	YES
LOUISIANA	YES

STATE	MANDATORY IMPRISONMENT
MAINE	YES
MARYLAND	YES
MASSACHUSETTS	YES
MICHIGAN	YES
MINNESOTA	YES
MISSISSIPPI	NO
MISSOURI	YES
MONTANA	YES**
NEBRASKA	YES
NEVADA	YES
NEW HAMPSHIRE	YES
NEW JERSEY	YES
NEW MEXICO	YES
NEW YORK	NO
NORTH CAROLINA	YES
NORTH DAKOTA	YES
OHIO	YES
OKLAHOMA	YES
OREGON	YES
PENNSYLVANIA	YES
RHODE ISLAND	YES

STATE	MANDATORY IMPRISONMENT
SOUTH CAROLINA	YES
SOUTH DAKOTA	NO
TENNESSEE	YES
TEXAS	YES
UTAH	YES
VERMONT	YES
VIRGINIA	YES
WASHINGTON	YES
WEST VIRGINIA	YES
WISCONSIN	YES
WYOMING	YES

*House arrest may be possible in lieu of a jail sentence.

**This sanction only applies to driving while under the influence offense.

Source: Mothers Against Drunk Driving (MADD).

STATES WITH OPEN CONTAINER LAWS

STATE	OPEN CONTAINER LAWS
ALABAMA	NO
ALASKA	YES*
ARIZONA	NO
ARKANSAS	NO
CALIFORNIA	YES
COLORADO	NO
CONNECTICUT	NO
DELAWARE	NO
DISTRICT OF COLUMBIA	YES
FLORIDA	YES
GEORGIA	YES*
HAWAII	YES
IDAHO	YES
ILLINOIS	YES
INDIANA	YES**
IOWA	YES*
KANSAS	YES
KENTUCKY	NO
LOUISIANA	NO

STATE	OPEN CONTAINER LAWS
MAINE	NO
MARYLAND	YES
MASSACHUSETTS	NO
MICHIGAN	YES
MINNESOTA	YES
MISSISSIPPI	NO
MISSOURI	NO
MONTANA	NO
NEBRASKA	NO
NEVADA	YES
NEW HAMPSHIRE	YES
NEW JERSEY	NO
NEW MEXICO	YES
NEW YORK	NO
NORTH CAROLINA	YES
NORTH DAKOTA	YES
OHIO	YES
OKLAHOMA	YES
OREGON	YES
PENNSYLVANIA	NO
RHODE ISLAND	NO

STATE	OPEN CONTAINER LAWS
SOUTH CAROLINA	YES
SOUTH DAKOTA	YES
TENNESSEE	YES*
TEXAS	NO
UTAH	YES
VERMONT	NO
VIRGINIA	NO
WASHINGTON	YES
WEST VIRGINIA	NO
WISCONSIN	YES
WYOMING	NO

*Applies only to drivers.
**Provided the driver has a BAC of 0.04 or higher.
Source: Mothers Against Drunk Driving (MADD).

GLOSSARY

GLOSSARY

Administrative License Revocation—A law which gives state officials the authority to suspend administratively the license of any driver who fails, or refuses to take, a BAC test.

Appearance—To come into court, personally or through an attorney, after being summoned.

Arraign—In a criminal proceeding, to accuse one of committing a wrong.

Arraignment—The initial step in the criminal process when the defendant is formally charged with the wrongful conduct.

Arrest—To deprive a person of his liberty by legal authority.

BAC—Blood alcohol concentration measured by the weight of the alcohol in a certain volume of blood.

Bail—Security, usually in the form of money, which is given to insure the future attendance of the defendant at all stages of a criminal proceeding.

Bail Bond—A document which secures the release of a person in custody, which is procured by security which is subject to forfeiture if the individual fails to appear.

Bench Warrant—An order of the court empowering the police or other legal authority to seize a person.

Burden of Proof—The duty of a party to substantiate an allegation or issue to convince the trier of fact as to the truth of their claim.

Capacity—Capacity is the legal qualification concerning the ability of one to understand the nature and effects of one's acts.

Commercial Driver License (CDL)—A license issued to an individual which authorizes that individual to drive a class of commercial motor vehicles.

Commissioner—Refers to the Commissioner of motor vehicles of a particular State.

Confession—In criminal law, an admission of guilt or other incriminating statement made by the accused.

Controlled Substance—All substances defined as illegal under the laws of the state, including any other drug or combination of other drugs to a degree which renders a person incapable of safely driving.

Conviction—An adjudication of guilt.

Court—The branch of government responsible for the resolution of disputes arising under the laws of the government.

Criminal Court—The court designed to hear prosecutions under the criminal laws.

Culpable—Referring to conduct, it is that which is deserving of moral blame.

Damages—In general, damages refers to monetary compensation which the law awards to one who has been injured by the actions of another, such as in the case of tortious conduct or breach of contractual obligations.

Deductible—An amount an insured person must pay before they are entitled to recover money from the insurer, in connection with a loss or expense covered by an insurance policy.

Defendant—In a civil proceeding, the party responding to the complaint.

Defense—Opposition to the truth or validity of the plaintiff's claims.

Department—Refers to the department of motor vehicles of a particular State.

District Attorney—An officer of a governmental body with the duty to prosecute those accused of crimes.

Docket—A list of cases on the court's calendar.

Drive—To drive, operate or be in actual physical control of a vehicle.

Driver—Every person who drives or is in actual physical control of a vehicle.

Driver's License—Any license to operate a motor vehicle issued under the laws of a particular state.

Due Process Rights—All rights which are of such fundamental importance as to require compliance with due process standards of fairness and justice.

Eyewitness—A person who can testify about a matter because of his or her own presence at the time of the event.

Family Purpose Doctrine—The doctrine which holds the owner of a family car liable in tort when it is operated negligently by another member of the family.

Felony—A crime of a graver or more serious nature than those designated as misdemeanors.

Forfeiture—The loss of goods or chattels, as a punishment for some crime or misdemeanor of the party forfeiting, and as a compensation for the offense and injury committed against the one to whom they are forfeited.

Hearing—A proceeding during which evidence is taken for the purpose of determining the facts of a dispute and reaching a decision.

Ignition Interlock—A device which has a breath tester that drivers blow into to measure their blood alcohol level and which, if alcohol is detected, prevent the vehicle from starting.

Illegal—Against the law.

Illegal Per Se—Illegal in and of itself.

Impound—To place property in the custody of an official.

Imprisonment—The confinement of an individual, usually as punishment for a crime.

Jail—Place of confinement where a person in custody of the government awaits trial or serves a sentence after conviction.

Judge—The individual who presides over a court, and whose function it is to determine controversies.

Jury—A group of individuals summoned to decide the facts in issue in a lawsuit.

Jury Trial—A trial during which the evidence is presented to a jury so that they can determine the issues of fact, and render a verdict based upon the law as it applies to their findings of fact.

Misdemeanor—Criminal offenses which are less serious than felonies and carry lesser penalties.

Motor Vehicle—Every vehicle which is self-propelled, and every vehicle which is propelled by electric power obtained from overhead trolley wires but not operated upon rails, except vehicles moved solely by human power and motorized wheelchairs.

No Fault Laws—The insurance laws which provide compensation to any person injured as a result of an automobile accident, regardless of fault.

Nonresident—Every person who is not a resident of the particular State.

Offense—Any misdemeanor or felony violation of the law for which a penalty is prescribed.

Owner—A person having the property in or title to a vehicle other than a lienholder.

Pain and Suffering—Refers to damages recoverable against a wrongdoer which include physical or mental suffering.

Pedestrian—Any person on foot.

Plea Bargaining—The process of negotiating a disposition of a case to avoid a trial of the matter.

Probable Cause—The standard which must be met in order for there to be a valid search and seizure or arrest. It includes the showing of facts and circumstances reasonably sufficient and credible to permit the police to obtain a warrant.

Prosecution—The process of pursuing a civil lawsuit or a criminal trial.

Prosecutor—The individual who prepares a criminal case against an individual accused of a crime.

Public Defender—A lawyer hired by the government to represent an indigent person accused of a crime.

Registration—The registration certificate and registration plates issued under the laws of the State pertaining to the registration of vehicles.

Revocation—The termination by formal action of a person's license or privilege to operate a motor vehicle on the highways, which terminated license or privilege shall not be subject to renewal or restoration except that an application for a new license may be presented and acted upon by the department after the expiration of the applicable period of time.

Search and Seizure—The search by law enforcement officials of a person or place in order to seize evidence to be used in the investigation and prosecution of a crime.

Summons—A mandate requiring the appearance of the defendant in an action under penalty of having judgment entered against him for failure to do so.

Suspension—The temporary withdrawal by formal action of a person's license or privilege to operate a motor vehicle on the public highways, which temporary withdrawal shall be for a period specifically designated.

Trial—The judicial procedure whereby disputes are determined based on the presentation of issues of law and fact. Issues of fact are decided by the trier of fact, either the judge or jury, and issues of law are decided by the judge.

Vehicle—Every device in, upon or by which any person or property is or may be transported or drawn upon a highway, excepting devices used exclusively upon stationary rails or tracks.

Verdict—The definitive answer given by the jury to the court concerning the matters of fact committed to the jury for their deliberation and determination.

Warrant—An official order directing that a certain act be undertaken, such as an arrest.

Warrantless Arrest—An arrest carried out without a warrant.

Zero Tolerance Laws—Laws which make it illegal for drivers under age 21 to drive with any measurable amount of alcohol in their system regardless of the BAC limit for older drivers.

BIBLIOGRAPHY

BIBLIOGRAPHY

Black's Law Dictionary, Fifth Edition. St. Paul, MN: West Publishing Company, 1979.

Campbell, James F, Fisher, P. David and Mansfield, David A.*Defense of Drunk Driving Cases.* New York, NY: Matthew Bender, 3d Edition, 1970 (Supp. 1999).

Insurance Institute for Highway Safety. (Date Visited: April 1999) http://www.hwysafety.org/

Mothers Against Drunk Driving (M.A.D.D.). (Date Visited: April 1999) http://www.madd.org/

National Highway Traffic Safety Administration. (Date Visited: April 1999) http://www.nhtsa.dot.gov/

Office of the Assistant Secretary for Public Affairs. (Date Visited: April 1999) http://www.dot.gov/briefing.htm/

United States Bureau of Transportation Statistics. (Date Visited: April 1999) http://www.bts.gov/

United States Department of Transportation. (Date Visited: April 1999) http://www.dot.gov/